THE ORIGINS OF
MODERN SPAIN

BY

J. B. TREND

New York
RUSSELL & RUSSELL
1965

FIRST PUBLISHED IN 1934

REISSUED, 1965, BY RUSSELL & RUSSELL, INC.

BY ARRANGEMENT WITH CAMBRIDGE UNIVERSITY PRESS

L.C. CATALOG CARD NO: 65—17925

PRINTED IN THE UNITED STATES OF AMERICA

J. A. B. P.

ἦ μεγάλα χάρις
δώρῳ σὺν ὀλίγῳ· πάντα δὲ τιματὰ τὰ πὰρ φίλων.

CONTENTS

PREFACE

The Origins of Modern Spain takes up the thread of the earlier chapters of *A Picture of Modern Spain*, published in 1921. Since then more material has accumulated, and the discovery that those chapters were quoted as authoritative in a well-known History of Spanish Literature encouraged me to make a closer study of the whole cultural and intellectual movement which began in 1868. Two friends who were with me in Spain in January 1931 and made the acquaintance of some of the younger members of the group, insisted that I should procrastinate no longer, and by the April of that year five chapters had been written practically as they stand to-day. Then came the proclamation of the Second Republic; and the question arose whether to hurry on with the book for that autumn, or to wait and watch developments. I chose the path of procrastination; and putting my book aside, I went back to Spain to see what was happening.

For various reasons I could not take up the manuscript again until the autumn of 1932. By that time the new situation in Spain had produced a number of books in English; but none of them touched my subject, except *Towards the New Spain* by Dr Joseph A. Brandt (University of Chicago Press)—a study of Castelar and the First Republic, which, if it had been published earlier, might have helped me considerably in my own second chapter. Like all students of modern Spain, I acknowledge a debt of gratitude to His Excellency Don Salvador de Madariaga for his *Spain* (1930) and *The Genius of Spain* (1923).

★   ★   ★

Though the form of the book is a collection of essays—intimate personal sketches of the reformers and educators of the generation of 1868—it deals with the whole movement, and in a more thorough manner than has been attempted before. Queen Isabella II is included as being what Spanish people call *contra-produciente*, i.e. having the opposite effect to that intended. She was hardly a reformer, poor dear; but her matronly figure and

her persuasive voice are essential to the background of Spain in
1868.
                    *   *   *

The book falls under four headings:
It begins with the intellectual and educational stagnation of
Spain before the revolution of 1868, and the "traditional
obstacles" which had previously buttressed that condition.

There had, however, been a dawn of intellectual liberty
before 1868—on the political side, French; on the philosophical
side, German; but on the cultural side, English.

The political movement led to the abortive revolution of
1868, the brief reign of Amadeo of Savoy, and the First Republic, which ended in the restoration of the Bourbons in 1875.

There remain the educational activities of those who had
failed in the attempt to make a new Spain at one blow during
the Interregnum, and the account of how they afterwards set
about evolving a new Spain by new methods, inspired largely
(though not exclusively) by English example. This forms the
greater part of the book.

                    *   *   *

Politics have been generally avoided, for my outlook is not
political, but educational. Questions of the monarchical or
republican forms of government, of clerical or lay teaching in
schools, are measured by their practical results on education in
Spain, not by their theoretical implications in an ideal State.

                    *   *   *

The list of Spanish friends to whom I am indebted would be
too long to print here. I can only mention Professor Antonio
Pastor (King's College, London) who paved my way with
introductions, Dr Alberto Giménez (Presidente de la Residencia de Estudiantes), the Master of my College in Madrid,
and Don Manuel B. Cossío, Director de la Institución Libre
de Enseñanza.

                                              J. B. T.

Cambridge
November 1933

There is nothing, however senseless it may be, which may not be true in this country, especially if it is against justice and the peace of mankind.

Pérez Galdós, *Los Duendes de la Camarilla*, ch. XXIX.

What? Miracles in my diocese, and without my permission? I forbid them, and if they continue they are of the devil.

A Bishop of Plasencia, quoted by Unamuno.

I

ESA SEÑORA
or that impossible Lady

THE ENGLAND of 1868 is a definite image. So too are the France of the Second Empire, the Germany of Wagner and Liszt, and the barely united kingdom of Italy, with Victor Emmanuel at Florence and Turin and Pio Nono reigning in a still Baroque Rome. Definite also in spite of their complexity are the United States at the end of the Civil War, and Uruguay, the Purple Land of W. H. Hudson. But Spain?

Seated on the throne of the Catholic kings, her portrait on the wall of every room in which two or three Spaniards are gathered together, is Isabella II, still under forty, still popular with the crowd through her pleasant smile and easy-going ways. Twenty years before, ten years before, the attachment of her subjects had been genuine and enthusiastic. To the people of Madrid she had seemed to be one of themselves. "She has all the Manolas to a woman", an English diplomat remarked to Greville in 1848, "and through them their lovers, brothers and friends; they would rise *en masse* if called upon."[1] By 1868, however, her popularity was on the wane; she was no longer respected by the more intelligent members of the public, while those who had had dealings with her in matters of government were reluctantly coming to the conclusion that she must go. *Esa señora es insuportable*, they were saying; that lady was impossible.

Yet women still had a good word for her, now and then. Pérez Galdós, the novelist, who may always be trusted to express the state of public opinion in Spain at any period of the nineteenth century, makes one of his characters put it in this way:

Only one person would be just, if they would let her, and that is the Queen. But they *don't* let her! They have got her in a regular

[1] Greville, *Memoirs*, 2nd Part, III, 119.

Chinese lantern of lies so that she can't see what's just or what's true; and so everything goes wrong.[1]

Isabella is married (that unfortunate affair of "the Spanish marriage"!) to her first cousin Don Francis of Assisi, Duke of Cadiz, a pathetic youth with a high, squeaky voice, known as "Paquita" (Fanny) and believed, by the Queen-mother and some of the diplomats, to be incapable of being a father. A "wretched imbecile sulky fanatic",[2] he had been known when on garrison duty at Pamplona to spend his leisure in a miniature chapel which he had had constructed in his quarters, dressing and undressing a holy image.

Much persuasion was necessary before Isabella would make up her mind in favour of "Fanny". "Well, I'll marry him if he's a man", she said at last, her downright and somewhat disconcerting manner made all the more equivocal by her beautiful southern voice. M. Bresson, the French minister, had been waiting in an anteroom. He was always in and out of the Palace, like a tradesman touting for orders, while his English colleague, Sir Henry Lytton Bulwer, lived like a gentleman in his country house at Aranjuez. It was after midnight[3]; but M. Bresson promptly obeyed the summons to congratulate the Queen—and prevent her from changing her mind.

"Paquita" was enchanted. He loved to see the young Queen (she was sixteen at the time) dressed in one sumptuous frock after another, so that he might admire the "law and poyze" of each winning movement, as she steered that plump but not ignoble frame before his enamoured eyes. Yet only a miracle, it was said, could make him a father. Isabella performed that miracle, and performed it no less than nine times. She was a vigorous and precocious young woman, by no means content to be a mere mannequin. Yet she caused a painful surprise, both to her consort and the diplomats, when four years later she showed signs that she was about to present the throne of Spain with an heir. Guizot, who had been chiefly responsible for the

[1] *Los Duendes de la Camarilla*, ch. XXIX.   [2] Greville, III, 48.

[3] Mr Bulwer to Lord Palmerston, in *The Letters of Queen Victoria* (First Series), II, 117.

marriage, was not at all surprised; he had expected it to happen before. *On a toujours dit que si nous ne nous hâtions pas, l'héritier viendrait avant le mari,* he had said to Greville.[1] But "Paquita" was deeply offended, mortified. He suffered from the strange delusion that the child was not his, and proposed to inform all the courts of Europe that he was not the father—a somewhat unusual interpretation of the traditional code of Spanish honour. He was anxious for a council to be summoned in order that he might lay before it proofs of the Queen's infidelity; and he even proposed to issue a manifesto to the Spanish nation on the subject. He was persuaded to desist from his scandalous intention.[2]

Poor "Paquita"! He had dreamed of a pure passion, quit of all earthly grossness; and now the bastard of some general or other (he thought) was to be foisted on him as his son! He expressed a wish for the dissolution of the marriage; but such a thing could not be considered for a moment. It was gravely debated (so at least the British minister was informed) whether the King-consort could not be quietly put out of the way with a cup of coffee, as being an easier and less scandalous way out of the difficulty.[3] Only with considerable tact could he be persuaded to return to the Palace.

And the diplomats! Where were all those schemes for assuring the succession of a French prince, schemes which had almost led to a rupture between France and England? France and Spain were to have become one again, as they had been in the eighteenth century, so closely united that when France sneezed, Spain was bound to answer "Jesús".[4] To what purpose had the marriage of the Queen's sister (the Infanta Luisa Fernanda) to the Duke of Montpensier been celebrated at the same time as the marriage of the Queen herself, in spite of the pledged word of Louis Philippe to Queen Victoria that it should take place at a later date? What, indeed, could have been better for the future of the Spanish monarchy than that the wilful,

---

[1] *Memoirs*, III, 32.　　　　　　　　　[2] *Ibid.* III, 78–9.
[3] Bulwer, *Palmerston*, III, 235–6.
[4] Proverb: *Cuando Francia estornuda, España dice ¡Jesús!*

extravagant, charitable Isabella should be succeeded by a prince whose father, the Duke of Montpensier, was so careful an administrator that he kept account of all the oranges sold from his garden in Seville, and was able when the moment came (and Isabella had gone) to finance even a revolution, so long as it seemed to offer a chance of putting himself on the throne?[1] Now everything had been upset, and the Queen after all might just as well have married the young man from Saxe-Coburg.

Legend relates that this Prince of the Asturias was brought out on a massive silver charger, to be shown to the King-consort and caressed by the ladies in waiting. Unfortunately the treatment was not beneficial, and the little prince died after two days.—Conveniently? So it was whispered, at any rate; for its survival would have removed the succession from the children of the Duke of Montpensier. The Queen in her grief vowed that on the next occasion there should be no silver dish, and that in future she would look after her children herself. This, however, is mere legend. The facts seem to be that the Queen's first child (born 12th July, 1850) died a few moments after its birth.[2] The "novel-reading public", however, founded on this melancholy occurrence the most horrible and absurd suppositions, which had to be contradicted publicly in the *Gazette* a few days later.[3] On 20th December, 1851, the silver dish duly appeared again.

Six weeks later (2nd February, 1852), as the Queen was leaving the Chapel Royal after giving thanks, an attempt on her life was made by a priest who stabbed her as he pretended to

[1] Cf. *La Flaca*, Barcelona, 6th Feb. 1870:

> Yo soy el rey naranjero
> De las huertas de Sevilla.
> Quise pillar un sillón,
> Y me quedé con la silla.

> I am the orange king
> Of the gardens of Seville (he said).
> I tried to sit on a throne,
> But was thrown on my seat instead.

[2] Condesa de Cerragería, *Apuntes de cronología y de historia de España*, 32.
[3] Cambronero, *Isabel II íntima*, 166 (note), prints the medical report.

present a petition. Subsequent examination showed that he had won a prize in a lottery and eked out his stipend by usury; but no motive for the crime was ever discovered, nor were there reprisals, attacks on priests or anticlerical riots. The Queen's popularity entered upon a new lease of life. Children continued to be born to her; but it was part of her tragic destiny—she has been called *La de los tristes destinos*—that only four of the nine survived. There were no baths in the Palace in those days. The windows were seldom opened. The royal family (so visitors observed) was not housed in the sunniest or airiest part of the building. There was something—it might have been the drains, if the magnificent eighteenth-century drains had been still in working order. "Rather 'niffy', those functions were, don't you know?" So they were described by a lady who attended them during the next reign.

Queen Isabella, unsteady and uneducated as she was, ignorant alike of bringing up a family and of ruling as a constitutional monarch, yet had "a good heart and noble instincts";[1] to which of the generals was it she said: "I have made you a duke, but I shall never succeed in making you a gentleman"? She also possessed a certain natural shrewdness and a truly Bourbon passion for intrigue. In matters of charity she was generous to a fault; she never knew the value of money, and her left hand never knew what her right was doing. But in matters of policy, her left hand knew only too well, and often regained by intrigue the concessions which the right had signed away. Her face, or at least her smile, might have been her fortune in the streets, as her voice was when she read her speeches from the throne. When she drove through Madrid from the Royal Palace to the gardens of Buen Retiro or the Church of Our Lady of Atocha, the compliments showered upon her were such as greet a pretty girl to-day, compliments—*piropos*—to which no nice girl would pay attention but which every intelligent girl would try to remember, whether she were aware of the picaresque implications or not. Isabella was fully aware of the picaresque implications; but her smile would only become more

[1] Bulwer, III, 236.

charming and more enigmatic, and she would nudge poor insignificant "Paquita" beside her in the carriage to make him sit up, smile and look pleasant. She liked to describe herself—and liked others to describe her—as *muy española*, very Spanish; and her tragedy was that of many of her own countrywomen. No day was hateful because she heard young men make naughty remarks about her as she passed by in the street; the hateful day was that on which no remarks were made any more, the day on which Isabella drove to the station at San Sebastian to catch the train for France.

Everything that was done in the Palace was done by backstairs influence. Direct action frightened the Queen. One of her earliest experiences (she was eleven at the time) had been an attempt to seize her on the part of two or three platoons of infantry and a dashing young general. The grand staircase was defended all night by eighteen halberdiers and their colonel; bullets frequently came through the shutters, and the plump little person of the Queen was only saved by making her lie down on the floor in a small apartment at the back. One or two bullets penetrated even as far as that.[1] It was a terrible experience. The general had to be shot, of course. She wanted to reprieve him, and for once she was wiser than her elders; for the execution of General Diego de León is now regarded as a political mistake.

Yet such direct attacks were, if anything, less dangerous than the normal procedure of the Palace. In the days of sheer absolutism the Prime Minister had been virtually a dictator. Even now, with the traditional Bourbon absolutism tempered by a struggling constitutional government, his power was little less, though it was softened and even endangered not, indeed, by Parliament but by the fear of plots within the Palace. Isabella was first the willing tool of the plotters and then their apt pupil. At the age of thirteen, when she had only just been declared

[1] Cambronero, 78–88, prints the original report on the occurrence drawn up by the Queen's governess, the Condesa de Espoz y Mina, an enlightened woman, afterwards the friend and helper of the prison-reformer, Concepción Arenal.

legally of age, she lent herself to a plot which drove her minister Olózaga into exile and destroyed the government which had been formed with such care and difficulty. The young Queen was apparently induced by the *camarilla* of plotters to make a serious charge against the Premier: that he had bolted the doors of her apartment, and then, by physical violence (catching hold of her dress and seizing her hand), had forced her to sign a decree to which she had objected. The story was obviously a fabrication; the doors had no bolts. Olózaga[1] persisted in his denial, while the Queen held by the declaration which she had made on the morning after, adding, however, the puzzling admission that she and her minister had parted on friendly terms and that she had given him a box of chocolates for his daughter. When questioned on the subject in later life, Isabella was uncertain what had happened about the decree, but she was quite certain about the chocolates.[2] Chocolates lay about on all the chairs in the Palace. Isabella realized the ambition of every child of her own age and her own time: If only I could be Queen for one day! The days grew to years, and Isabella grew up. She was Queen, but she was never Queen over her passions. "A safe word whispered by a crawling confessor, an attack of nerves on a cloudy day, the appearance of a well-made soldier at a levee, have often sufficed to make and break administrations."[3]

The politics of the Palace were the politics of the bedchamber and the private chapel. Behind the throne stood Father Claret, the Queen's confessor, and Sor Patrocinio, in whose hands and feet were the marks of the wounds of Christ. Father Claret, in spite of his name,[4] had to be taken seriously, even by the superficial and heretical English, for his time and talents were by no means fully occupied in hearing the Queen's confessions.

[1] Olózaga was the inventor of the phrase "the traditional obstacles", a formula which, as long as it remains undefined, is elastic and convenient.

[2] Pérez Galdós, *Memoranda*, 20.

[3] John Hay, *Castilian Days*, 357.

[4] Ven. Antonio María Claret y Clará, 1807–70. He was declared *venerable* by Leo XIII on the 4th Dec. 1899.

Moreover, he had been an archbishop in Cuba, and was now titular bishop of Trajanopolis *in partibus infidelium*. To his credit it may be said that, as President of the Escurial, he was responsible for planting ten thousand fruit trees—which failed to grow. Politically he was the greatest of the "traditional obstacles", and at the revolution of 1868 he was attacked more fiercely than the Queen. He had led her into temptation, it was declared, and his relations with Sor Patrocinio were neither clear nor holy. His portrait,[1] with the thick, sensual lips and the expression of cunning thinly veiled by a somewhat bovine simplicity, makes it possible to believe him capable of anything.

Sor Patrocinio, the "Bleeding Nun", although she had been prosecuted for fraud, as many saints in former centuries had been prosecuted by the Holy Inquisition,[2] had regained her position through sheer force of personality. Her miraculous pretensions were described by a dignitary of the Church as "a farce unworthy of a catholic nation"; but it is significant that that prelate received no higher preferment, while the doctor who had once healed her wounds was afterwards punished for his offence. The stigmata were discreetly veiled from view by mittens; but the wax-white mittened fingers were in every pie. Her power over the Queen was incalculable. With Father Fulgencio, a predecessor of Father Claret, she had succeeded on at least one occasion in upsetting a ministry for no apparent reason, putting in its place one which, though it lasted only a few hours, included so many nonentities that it brought the Crown into ridicule. Galdós has described a scene of the same kind later in the reign; it actually took place in 1865, but is characteristic of the prevailing methods of government.

Suddenly, when no one was expecting it, the government fell. *Quare causa?* No one knew; and what was worse, no one asked. We had become accustomed to governments coming and going for no other reason than the whims and fancies of the Señora. That lady was

[1] Cambronero, 262.
[2] *E.g.* the Beata de Soto, Magdalena de la Cruz, María de la Visitación, Luisa de la Asunción, Francisca Martín. H. C. Lea, *The Religious History of Spain*, 416–20.

certainly confused and embittered just then by the news brought from Paris by the King-consort who had been to pay a visit to the Empress Eugénie. Napoleon and his wife had given him a dressing-down for the obstinacy with which Spain refused to recognize the kingdom of Italy, a *fait accompli* which no country in Europe could consider as non-existent and remain within the comity of nations. The conduct of Spain was intolerable Quixotism. This, more or less, was what they had said to Don Francis of Assisi; and in the same form as they had urged it upon him, he passed it on to his spouse. She, however, raised her hands in horror, repeating in a trembling, frightened voice: "But we can't! We *can't*!"

Isabel II communicated immediately with her guardian angels Sor Patrocinio and Father Claret, reporting the dire communication which Don Francis of Assisi had brought from Paris. It is reported that both reverend personages pursed their lips and knitted their brows. Let Napoleon rule in his own house and leave our gracious Queen to govern in hers! Spain should remain firm in her decision relating to the so-called kingdom of Italy, and with the protection of the Virgin she had nothing to fear from the concert or disconcert of Europe....

"Narváez."

"Señora?"

"I want you now, more than ever. I have dismissed Mon. Make me any ministry you like; I don't mind what you do so long as it doesn't involve the recognition of Italy...."

Narváez took the helm of the leaking ship of state.

Some little apologies for elections were held.... But...it wouldn't do. Narváez must go. She came to this conclusion two days before the opening of the new Cortes; and as she thought, so she did, offended and mortified. Narváez had decided on the evacuation of Santo Domingo, the only possible way out of a long and expensive war....

"Istúriz."

"Señora?"

"Narváez has deceived me; I must do without him. Besides, I do not agree to the evacuation of Santo Domingo. You will form me a ministry with unionist elements...."

"*I*, Señora, *I*...?"

The illustrious old man who had served the Spanish monarchy so well, both in politics and diplomacy, hesitated between his respect for the Queen and his dislike of lending himself once more to such pastry-cook's work in public.... But the excuses with which his modesty and weariness would have eluded the task were of no avail; her exquisite amiability and the sweetness of her manner overcame him.

"Not at all. Not at all. I ask you this as a favour and you are not going to deny me. To-morrow, at this time, you will bring me the list of your ministry."

When the twenty-four hours were past, good old Don Javier arrived at the Palace with the list of the new ministers.

"Are they all there? Let's see.... Good. I agree. What time is it? Twelve? Well, at three o'clock punctually they may come and take the oath."

But by a quarter to three she had changed her mind.

"Istúriz."

"Señora?"

"That's all settled. Narváez has been here, and oh! what things he told me! But we will leave all that for another time."

Leave it for another time! He breathed again.[1]

In after years the Queen defended the memory of Sor Patrocinio, more generously, perhaps, than sincerely. "She was a very good woman," she said to Pérez Galdós when he was presented to her in Paris, "a good woman and a saint; she did not meddle with politics or things to do with the government. She did intervene, certainly, in the affairs of my family, so that my husband and I should make it up; but nothing more. Idle people have invented whole catalogues of things which have gone all over Spain and all round the world....Of course, that change of ministry was a mistake, but it was all put right the next day...."[2]

Yet Isabella II, in spite of her protests, had a greater intimacy with nuns than was altogether wise for a crowned head in the nineteenth century. She could turn all men round her little finger, but she herself was clay in the hands of any member of a

[1] Pérez Galdós, *Prim*, ch. XI.　　[2] Pérez Galdós, *Memoranda*, 21.

religious order. Of Madre Sacramento, for instance, she could write as follows:

13 April 1890.

...To the inexpressible consolation of my soul I acceded to her wishes and her repeated demands, and discontinued the practice of attending religious functions in a low-necked dress....

Sr Claret, my confessor, who was also confessor to Micaela [Madre Sacramento], told me that she was a great saint; and he used to send for her to come to the Palace on account of the great spiritual good she did me. This opinion was confirmed by my seeing how she guessed everything that went on within me, as if I myself had told her.[1]

Madre Sacramento had died in her convent at Valencia, nursing her sisters during an outbreak of cholera. Sor Patrocinio lived to a green old age to carry on her work. If anything had to be done, any delicate piece of negotiation to be carried out, Sor Patrocinio was the person to approach. If there was a young friend who had been caught in the street fighting during the last insurrection and was now in jail awaiting transportation, or an old friend who had been involved in the last military revolt and was lying wounded in some attic nursed by a devoted mistress, the only way to prevent the law from taking its course was a word in the right quarter from Sor Patrocinio. *La Madre*, she was called by those who knew her; for she had been for many years Mother Superior of a fashionable convent in Madrid. "Never", exclaims John Hay, a thoughtful and clear-sighted American who was attached to the United States Legation in 1870,[2] "in all the darkest periods of Spanish history, was the reign of superstition so absolute and tyrannical as in the Alcázar of Madrid during the later years of Isabel of Bourbon."[3] Sor Patrocinio could tell the most astonishing stories of her life in the cloister. The devil used to come swooping down on bat-like wing, and take her for an airing above the house-tops of the

[1] Cerragería, 132.
[2] He had been private secretary to Lincoln, and was part author of a monumental life of his chief.
[3] *Castilian Days*, 225–6.

capital; on one occasion he carried her as far as the passes over the Guadarrama, leaving her sitting on the convent roof. In the Palace, her principal duty was to sanctify by a day's wearing the more intimate garments of her royal mistress and friend, Isabella II.

Pérez Galdós, whose historical novels have been proved to rest on a solid documentation and who had an unerring instinct for knowing what the sober citizen of Madrid thought of all that went on, has reported a conversation which shows what Spanish women thought of Sor Patrocinio when her reputation was at its highest. Lucila, who has been nursing a wounded officer wanted by the police, is talking to her friend Domiciana, an ex-cloistered nun:

"Do you really like her?" asks Lucila. "That must be because she has been good to you. And do you believe in her wounds too?"

"How can I believe in her wounds if I know how they're made! Sometimes she has asked me to make them again when they were healing. I know the secret; the nun who showed Patrocinio how it was done showed me too....Yes, yes, I know how to make stigmata. It's quite easy. Clematis, you know; what people here call 'Beggar's herb'. I've got some. Would you like to try? You'll see how quickly...."

"No, thank you. That is not the way in which it has pleased God to call me."

"Nor me, either. That's why it never occurred to me to make the stigmata on myself. The reasons which Patrocinio had for making them were of a higher order, and it is not for us to say whether she was doing right or wrong. Things which would be bestial, sinful, and even sacrilegious in people like you and me may be good, necessary, and even indispensable in other people, who are called to great things by the merits of their understanding and will. What d'you say? I don't believe you understand a word of what I'm saying, little silly!"

"Well, Domiciana, I always think straight in front of me. I believe that things which are bad when I do them must be bad in queens and empresses too."

"I don't agree. You're an idiot; you don't know the world....I can vouch for the great gifts and faculties which the Lord has given to Patrocinio. There's no woman like her."[1]

At last the day came when Isabella II went. "That lady" had become impossible. The September revolution caught her on her summer holiday, away in the Basque provinces. All the generals deserted her but one; an admiral arranged for the Spanish exiles to return by sea to Cadiz. A guard of honour of loyal engineers saw her across the French frontier.

That was in 1868. Eleven years later, having abdicated and taken up her residence in Paris, she returned to Madrid on a short visit for the second marriage of her son, Alfonso XII. From the first marriage she had naturally absented herself; Queen Mercedes had been the daughter of that intriguing fruiterer, the Duke of Montpensier. "It is a curious fact", the United States minister, James Russell Lowell, reported to his government, "that the ex-Queen was received wherever she showed herself in public with the most noisy demonstrations of popularity, in marked contrast with the silence with which her son and his Austrian bride were received. This was partly, no doubt, intended to heighten the emphasis of the public in-difference towards them, but it was also a proof of her personal popularity, which is still very great in spite of all her faults and follies, and perhaps it might be said in consequence of them."[2]

Pérez Galdós may help us to understand why. Though a man of distinctly republican sympathies, he was received by Isabella on two separate occasions in Paris; and he has left a most interesting portrait of her as an old lady, when the comings and goings of that noble frame were steered by a knotted stick. What attracted him most about her was her way of speaking. As a novelist, it fascinated him for reasons of literary technique; as a historical novelist, author of some forty or fifty volumes of "Episodios Nacionales", it was beyond the price of many documents. "How did Santa Teresa speak?" asks Azorín in one of his essays. "What was her voice like?" And we realize in a

---

[1] *Los Duendes de la Camarilla*, ch. VI.
[2] James Russell Lowell, *Impressions of Spain*, 102–3.

flash that the secret of her power lay not so much in her visions as in her voice. What would one not give to hear the actual voices of the great characters in history? Galdós had the supreme good fortune to hear the actual voice of one of his own characters in fiction.

He was duly presented by the ambassador, and Isabella, "with an exquisite kindliness" and "an amiability which had about it much that was domestic", at once treated him as one of the family, as indeed she had been accustomed to treat all Spanish people, regarding them one and all as members of the *casa nacional*, the national home. She addressed him in the second person singular, and made the somewhat shy republican feel perfectly at home, although not two minutes before, he had wanted to run away.

Doña Isabel spoke distinctly, and in a way that was characteristically Spanish, making frequent use of rapid, idiomatic phrases such as were common in the older forms of the language. She had no trace of a foreign accent, and no foreign notions peeped out through the thickly-woven texture of her Spanish ideas. Her language was, in fact, strictly middle-class and rather old-fashioned, although without archaisms, the language spoken in the first half of the last century by educated women—educated, but not necessarily aristocratic. The Queen's manner of speech was formed, no doubt, in that circle of women, some drawn from the nobility and others servants, who surrounded her and whose conversation she heard, in her infancy and at the beginning of her reign.[1]

"I will tell you lots of things," she said, "lots; some, that you may write them down; others, that you may know about them."

How far away all this seems now—a Ruritania without an Anthony Hope!

Spain in the time of Isabella II, when contemplated from the serene and tranquil heights of the nineteen-thirties, seems more

---

[1] Pérez Galdós, *Memoranda*, 18–19.

like a madhouse than the inheritance of some of the greatest
makers of civilization. Even the Portuguese were in the habit of
referring to Spain as "the madhouse over the border", and that
impression could be strengthened from the observations of
political historians. Spanish political history in this period
appears as a comic opera in which every scene ends in tragedy;
the players might have been more at home in comedy, but they
are compelled, unexpectedly and somewhat reluctantly, to take
tragic parts. Only when we leave the governors and try to be
on the side of the governed, when we endeavour to regard
events from a Spanish point of view, does the history of the
time begin to make sense, and the most senseless-seeming
actions appear to have a cause if not always an explanation.

Some of these causes are to be found in the fantastic, tragic,
futile reign of Isabella II; but the source of the trouble is older
than that. Since the death of Philip II in 1599 there has been
only one Spanish king of real capacity: Charles III, who reigned
from 1759 to 1788. Even so, his great constructive work and
the work of the ministers he so ably chose was rapidly undone
in the reaction of the reign which followed, and Charles IV
(1788–1808) is only remembered now as the successful—and
absurd—model of a great painter, Goya. Since the time of
Charles III, the heads on which the Spanish crown has rested
have had little capacity for governing and still less for understanding the obligations of a constitutional monarch. The value
of truth, the rights of the individual conscience, the iniquity of
persecution—such thoughts and feelings as these have either lain
beyond their understanding, or have been carefully kept from
their knowledge. Moreover, the fault was not entirely with the
royal tutors or royal governesses; those who had charge of
Isabella were many of them excellent, but how could they be
expected to do anything with a girl whose mother and aunts
were like the mother and aunts of Isabella II? The failure
was not so much the fault of the crowned heads as their
misfortune; the surroundings and traditions of the Spanish
throne, to say nothing of the medical history of Isabella II—the
offspring of Ferdinand VII and one of his nieces—seem to have

made any thorough or intellectual grasp of the problems of government impossible. The quality which strikes Spanish observers in members of the House of Bourbon is their incurable, criminal lack of seriousness.

In 1868 (as in 1931) there were many who favoured the revolution not because they were anti-monarchist but because they were anti-Bourbon. They saw what the surroundings of Spanish royalty were, and the nature and complexion of the "traditional obstacles". With a weak and wayward woman like Isabella, the triumph of those traditions and those obstacles was not surprising; their strength was to be revealed even more clearly by their power to make the position untenable for a strong, upright man like Amadeo of Savoy, who, after a brief interregnum, succeeded her in 1870.

II

THE FIRST REPUBLIC
or Honesty not the best Policy

T HE INTERREGNUM, from the departure of Isabella II, in September, 1868, to the restoration of the Bourbons with Alfonso XII, in January, 1875, is sometimes described as "the black years". That at any rate is the label applied to it in the text-book of an ancient English university. These years were not "black" in the usual sense of the word; Spain was far more "black" after the restoration in 1875. Martin Hume preferred the epithet "red"; he could never mention the republic without calling it the "red" republic. Black or red, it was not proclaimed at once. From 1868 until 1870 there was a provisional government; from 1870 until 1873 the throne was occupied by Amadeo of Savoy. The republic was not proclaimed until his abdication (11th February, 1873) and it was ended on the 3rd January, 1874 (as governments in Spain have often ended in the nineteenth century), by a general and a handful of soldiers.

That particular general is something of a mystery, for he was (so his defenders say) a republican, or at least anti-Bourbon, and he got n thing out of his *pronunciamiento* for himself. His name was I vía—José Manuel Pavía y Rodríguez de Albuquerque—and he should not be confused with another distinguished general of the name of Pavía—Manuel Pavía y Lacy, Marqués de Novaliches—who lost the battle of Alcolea in the autumn of 1868 and had his beard shot away in the service of Isabella II. The *Annual Register* states that this officer died of wounds two days after the battle; but a later authority encourages the belief that he lived to a green old age and died in 1896. As his mother's name was Lacy, he may have been half English, or half Irish.

His namesake, who afterwards ended the republic by dissolving the Cortes by force and occupying the House of

Parliament with troops, is claimed to have been a perfectly honest man, with somewhat confused notions of politics. He had enough sense of public duty to realize that something ought to be done, and thought that he was the man to do it—the argument of all would-be dictators. But General Pavía y Rodríguez de Albuquerque was not like other dictators. Having dissolved Parliament in the regulation military manner, he summoned a council of notables, told them to form a government, and then retired into private life. He was nicknamed *La flor de un día* (the flower of a day); neither his friends nor his enemies could ever understand why he had made nothing out of it. It was left for another general, Martínez Campos, to "pronounce" in favour of Alfonso XII; he made his *pronunciamiento* on the historic site of Saguntum, on the 24th December, 1874, and it may be added that he did very well out of it and did not immediately retire into private life. If General Pavía y Rodríguez de Albuquerque were really as exceptional as his admirers pretend, it would be tempting to inquire whether he may not have come under the influence of Sanz del Río and the philosophic radicals, the reformers of 1868, or have been reached by George Borrow and the colporteurs of the Bible Society. There is no evidence, so far as can be ascertained, for either the one supposition or the other; nor can his "spleen" be explained, as it can in the case of the other General Pavía, on the supposition that his mother was English or Irish. The surname Pavía y Rodríguez de Albuquerque shows quite clearly that she was not. The source of his anti-Bourbon sentiments was probably the same as that of the anti-Bourbon sentiments of General Prim—the Impossible Lady herself. The beginnings of another movement of the same kind may be seen in the rising at Seville (in August, 1932) of General Sanjurjo, who, like General Pavía y Rodríguez de Albuquerque, was a good soldier with somewhat confused notions of politics, and he too turned out to be the flower of a single day.

The English historians of the Interregnum have not been sympathetic; they have not even been impartial. Butler Clarke aimed at the most scrupulous fairness, but even he refused to take seriously a factor which is of the utmost importance in southern countries—and in northern countries also, except England—the factor of oratory. All politicians may be windbags; political leaders must be. There has been oratory before now in English politics, and there may be again. Oratory is not merely a "Latin" characteristic; the Dutch and the Norwegians, unemotional peoples from a Latin standpoint, can be untiring speakers when the occasion demands it, and the occasion seems to demand it considerably more often than it does in modern England. Yet even in England, ideals, if they are to be expressed, must be expressed in words—in that choice of plain words which, in Spain, may seem to the last degree cold and unsympathetic, and which a Spanish writer has called "rhetoric in a minor key". English writers, in deprecating the rhetoric of the republican leaders in Spain, both then and now, have not made allowances for the language; and in discounting the rhetoric they have also discounted the ideals.

Spanish republicanism is descended from the liberalism sown in Spain by the French Revolution. In fighting the French, the leaders of the Spanish national movement could not fail to learn something of those mysterious and convincing political ideals which gave the French armies their "peculiar momentum". The Peninsular War (as the Warden of New College has pointed out) was a school of politics. "It taught Spaniards that they could live without a king; it revived the old provincial feeling; it led to the spread of democratic ideas in the towns and in the army; it restored the lost tradition of the Cortes."[1]

Reliable witnesses for the events of that time are not easy to find. The British minister at Madrid for the greater part of the period was Sir Henry Layard, the excavator of Nineveh; his published letters unfortunately stop short with his appointment to Madrid. It is known, at any rate, that the British Legation became once more a city of refuge for fallen ministers; and the Layards are said to have saved the life of General Serrano, "the pretty general" (*el general bonito*), who was at that time Regent, by conveying him in disguise to Santander, whence he took

[1] H. A. L. Fisher, *The Republican Tradition in Europe*, 258.

ship for St Jean de Luz and escaped from Spain at a critical and (for himself) highly dangerous moment.

A more impartial witness to the progress of the revolution would have been John Hay, Abraham Lincoln's former secretary and future biographer; but Hay's writings on Spain do not go beyond 1870, and his actual account of the first Spanish republic was never published at all. He at any rate could contemplate the possibility of a republic in Spain without misgivings. His own republic had just passed, and passed triumphantly, through the test of the Civil War. His observations on Spain in 1870 are invaluable as an unbiased record of public feeling.

Let us however first hear the Spanish side—in the words of Francisco Giner:

In few periods of contemporary history had the younger generation nourished such high hopes as during the ten years before the revolution of September 1868.... The nation, indignant as it seemed, at the older ways—though in reality (as we saw afterwards) merely tired of the old names, sought among the new generation for the champions of its honour and liberty.... The September Revolution was consummated. The old régime fell, and with it disappeared almost all the men who, some from loyalty, others from treachery, most from blindness and all from egoism—either for their parties or themselves—had only served the government in order to prolong its agony. Upon ruins such as these were proclaimed those principles which, reasonably or not, constitute the rights of modern peoples: liberty in worship, education and the press; inviolability of domicile; personal security (from unjustifiable arrest); abolition of capital punishment, slavery, conscription and official monopolies; the introduction of universal suffrage, trial by jury, and popular election of the members of both houses.[1]

By the beginning of 1870 it really seemed to an impartial observer like John Hay that "the tyranny of tradition" was losing its power. A great deal (he considered) had been accomplished by the single act of driving out the Queen. That was "a

[1] *Obras*, vIII, 101–3.

blow at superstition" which gave the whole body politic a most salutary shock. Never before in Spain had a revolution been directed at the throne. Before, it had always been an obnoxious ministry that was to be driven out; the monarch remained, and the exiled outlaw of to-day might be Premier to-morrow.[1] Many people, also, had grown weary of a system "which repressed all freedom of thought and rights of conscience, and which placed the education of the young in the hands of the Jesuits"; they hailed with delight a decree issued by the Minister of Justice suppressing the Jesuit order throughout Spain and the Spanish Islands, requiring its colleges and in-stitutions to be closed within three days and declaring its movable and immovable property sequestrated to the State.[2] The law of civil marriage, after a desperate struggle in the Cortes, had gone into operation with general assent; and there was a large party which actively favoured the entire separation of the spiritual from the temporal power, "making religion voluntary and free, and breaking its long concubinage with the Crown". The "old superstition", it was true, still hung like a fog over the country, but it was invaded by flashes and rays of progress. It could not (John Hay thought) resist much longer the sunshine of a more tolerant age.

The revolution of September, 1868, however, had not made the progress that its sanguine friends had desired. There were still too many generals; and the generals left no one long in doubt as to their real intentions, which were to re-establish the monarchy—as a constitutional monarchy, of course—*a la inglesa*, on the English model. The provisional government elected a monarchical Cortes and framed a monarchical con-stitution. They crushed republican risings in Cadiz and Catalonia, and promptly shot "such impatient patriots as it could find". The provisional government was hard pressed from the beginning. The Carlist war broke out afresh; "bands of hardy mountaineers roved about the provinces of Biscay, Álava, Guipúzcoa and Navarre, burning railway stations, upsetting trains, cutting telegraph wires, levying

[1] *Castilian Days*, 71.　　　[2] *Annual Register* (1868), 212.

contributions, and otherwise keeping the peaceable inhabitants in terror".

Meanwhile the provisional government had been unofficially offering the crown of the Catholic kings to all the unemployed princes within the reach of its diplomacy. Queen Victoria had heard, as early as the 9th October, of the probability of the offer of the throne of Spain to an English prince, and had informed Mr Disraeli that she could not consent to its being entertained for a moment.

"Her Majesty", General Grey wrote to Lord Stanley, "would see with much reluctance, under any circumstances, a throne from which another family had been ejected, occupied by one of her children." But in the case of Spain (it was added) there were many reasons which made it most undesirable that the offer of the crown, if made, should be accepted by an English prince. Queen Victoria's shrewd common sense enabled her to foresee only too clearly what would happen, and did actually happen in the case of Amadeo of Savoy. "Different Parties in Spain may combine to overthrow the Throne of Queen Isabella; but does our experience of Spanish Statesmen warrant the hope, that, their object effected, they will continue to act in harmony, or agree amongst themselves as to the Government to be set up? The Spaniards, besides, are proverbially indisposed to foreigners; so that an English Prince, accepting the offer of the Crown in the present circumstances, would probably find himself supported by one part of the nation, and violently opposed by another, and would thus become the cause of fresh Civil wars and calamities in that unhappy country. The Queen need not say how much it would distress her to see one of her sons in such a position. Then the jealousy of France...."[1]

The proposed candidature of a Roman Catholic Hohenzollern (Prince Leopold of Hohenzollern-Sigmaringen) was one of the immediate causes of the Franco-Prussian War. A formal offer to the veteran General Espartero was unfortunately refused, and eventually the choice fell upon Prince

[1] *The Letters of Queen Victoria* (Second Series), I, 540.

Amadeo of Savoy, Duke of Aosta. It was a wretched business. Cold-shouldered by the "black" clerical aristocracy, as being an enemy of the Pope, and coming from "the so-called Kingdom of Italy"; deprived of his staunchest supporter, Prim, who was murdered a day or two before he landed; at the mercy of all the traditional obstacles and intrigues, with the peculiar horrors of a Carlist war raging once more in the north-east, and Cuba in a perpetual state of unrest or rebellion, no foreign prince could have succeeded, however upright, honest, public-spirited or strictly constitutional.

Moreover Amadeo was an Italian; and for that reason alone he fell a victim to the ridicule with which, for some unknown reason, most Spaniards regard Italians (and, it may be added, most Italians regard Spaniards); a misunderstanding which is one of the most unfortunate in Europe and which, being founded on ridicule, is one of the most difficult to cure. Many good monarchists had turned against Isabella, when they heard that she had taken, as her latest lover, Marfori her steward, the son of an Italian pastrycook. The harm lay not so much in the existence of yet another lover, nor even in his being the son of a pastry-cook, as in the fact that the lover was an Italian. Amadeo was also an Italian. The Spanish people, with whom a sense of humour is almost a disease, could never forget that in the moment of solemnity and emotion when the new king swore to obey the constitution, he had mispronounced the word "I swear"; he had said *giuro* as in Italian instead of *juro* with the distinctive Spanish *j*. The story may be a pure invention; it is probably a traditional joke against all Italians speaking Spanish, a joke so old and deeply rooted that no one in Spain will ever believe or admit that an Italian, however well he may speak Spanish, can possibly pronounce *juro* in any other way than *giuro*. In the same way, a number of Spanish people will never admit that an Englishman can use any part of the Spanish verb except the infinitive; if the inaccuracy of the belief is demonstrated, the reply will probably be: "You are the only Englishman I have ever heard do so". An English or a German prince, then, would have suffered the same ridiculous mishap as did

Amadeo; whatever he had really said when swearing to obey the constitution would have been reported in the comic papers as *Yo jurar*, and his reign would have been prejudiced from the beginning as was the disastrous two-years' reign of Amadeo of Savoy.

On the abdication of Amadeo, a republic was proclaimed. It never had a chance. Let us, for once, instead of repeating the abuse which is regularly showered on it by English historians, publicists and propagandists, endeavour to see it through Spanish eyes—through the eyes of a moderate man whose name is known all over the world wherever the Spanish language is read or spoken, the gentle essayist, Azorín:

"The republic of 1873!" he exclaims, "that republic which was an accumulation of horrors; that republic which offered the whole of Spain the spectacle of disorder, with every kind of outrage and injustice! Conservatives, friends of the past, passionately devoted to tradition, are unwilling to learn their history when it comes to the republic of 1873. It is useless to tell them that this republic really existed. With a disdainful smile, they merely go on talking as before.

"The republic of 1873 had a vice in its origin which incapacitated it from the very first; it was born of Cortes that were not republican but monarchist, composed of elements which called themselves republican but were monarchist at heart; throughout its existence it had to struggle within itself. These conditions made it impossible for the republic to develop in the normal way. In addition to two wars, with which it was faced from the beginning, the Carlist war and the war in Cuba, it had to cope with supporters who were republican only in name.

"The republican party in Spain was federal. It had been born federal, and there was no other republican party in Spain than this. Yet the republic which came forth from a monarchist chamber and had to meet the attacks of monarchist enemies, was centralist, unitary. The ideal of republican opinion was federation; for federalism, and in defence of individual rights, the party had risen to arms in 1869, and had had its heroes, like young Froilán Carvajal, who cried 'Viva la república!' in front of the soldiers who were taking aim to shoot him. For federation, also, republicans and socialists had fought together on the same side.

"And now that the republic was there, it did not belong to the republicans but to the monarchists. Republicans and socialists saw themselves defrauded of their aspirations, and the ideals which they had maintained and cherished all their life long, vanish into thin air. Socialists were excluded from the government, and the federal system postponed. And militarism, which had annulled all previous revolutions, and which now provided monarchist generals in whom the republic ingenuously placed its confidence—militarism ended by annulling the republic as well, and a general dissolved the legislative assembly."

When those words were written (in March, 1931) it had yet to be proved whether or not a republic was practicable in Spain. At the present moment, the best brains in the country seem to agree that it is practicable, and have been proving since April, 1931, that it will work quite as well, and generally a great deal better than the old monarchy. Spain has never had a truly constitutional monarchy, a *monarquía a la inglesa*. The revolution of 1931 was made in order to obtain, by means of a republican form of government, civil liberties comparable with those enjoyed by Great Britain, Holland, Belgium, Denmark, Sweden and Norway, under constitutional monarchy.

The conditions of 1873 were so exceptional that they proved nothing against the republican form of government in Spain—not even, perhaps, that federalism was a mistake, but merely, that it may have been applied too hastily or in the wrong way. Nor was the gentle Pi y Margall, the apostle of federalism, by any means the "unspeakable intellectual" that some writers would have us believe. Pi y Margall was a man who had been persecuted for his faith. In youth he had written a *History of Spanish Painting* which (for some reason or other) had been condemned by the Church and prohibited by a Royal Order; while the publication of his *Studies of the Middle Ages* had brought upon their author the ban of excommunication. In 1874, when he was no longer President of the Spanish Republic —when, indeed, there was no longer a republic in Spain—a priest had tried to assassinate him; and his friends remembered that it was a priest, too, who had stabbed Queen Isabella, and priests who had murdered the republican Civil Governor of Burgos in the very precincts of the cathedral.

The federal programme, in spite of its obvious drawbacks, seemed to have more substance than the others, even after the restoration had removed all hope of its being put into practice. The apostle of federalism was a man whose austerity and virtue could serve as a permanent example to future generations, and citizens who took kindly to ideas of justice and liberty declared themselves federals, not through having thought at all deeply on the meaning, methods or objects of federalism—a system which not even the "Margallists" could always explain—but from the knowledge that these were the views held by a man of the un-blemished personal character of Pi y Margall.[1] It was all the same to them whether they understood the real meaning of the federation which Pi defended; the immense majority of the federalists would probably have been centralists or imperialists, if either of these had been the position of the master. Neither was it of great consequence whether they understood the real meaning of the pact proposed by Pi, "synallagmatic, commuta-tive and bilateral"; nor had many of them so much as opened his book on nationalities. The only thing which interested the Spanish federalists was the man who said these things; and he would have been equally respected if he had dispensed with the parade of philosophical learning with which those ideas appeared in his books. "They admired the man whose life was as clear as crystal, whose honesty persisted through all his mis-fortunes; and they knew, besides, that his private life corre-sponded, in its inflexible purity, to his action in politics. The individual, quite apart from his doctrine, was an object of faith to many thousands of Spaniards who awaited, in messianic expectation, the regeneration of their country through him." But Pi was no politician. He was a man of definitions, a man of pure thought; less profound than Salmerón, but infinitely more

[1] H. R. Romero Flores, *Reflexiones sobre el alma y el cuerpo de la España actual*, 27-30.

accessible. For that reason, the formidable movement of opinion which he succeeded in creating was paralysed from its birth; "and instead of expressing itself in civic action in proportion to the force of its impulse, it had hardly any consequences in the life of the Spanish nation, other than those produced by the tone of professional honesty which was common to all the federalists".

Francisco Giner believed that federalism was inadvisable in Spain, and at any rate impracticable under the actual conditions; and his friend Nicolás Salmerón rose to be President of the Republic as the leader of those who desired a centralized state as opposed to a federal one. Salmerón governed from the 18th July to the 7th September. Even to not over-sympathetic foreign observers, he seemed different from those who had preceded him—different because he was more straightforward. The ethical teaching of Sanz del Río and the friendship of Francisco Giner had not been without their effect. Salmerón's predecessor, Pi y Margall, had not made a good impression, least of all on foreign observers. Pi y Margall had been too doctrinaire; his extreme federal ideas were having disastrous consequences in the south, where every town wished to be an independent canton, and Cartagena (the naval base) had gone "red" and had a fleet of its own. One English historian refers to Pi y Margall as "unspeakable"; and we turn from him to an essay by Azorín,[1] and watch a little old man and a little old woman, looking like country cousins in their best clothes with a smell of camphor on them, visiting an exhibition of pictures in Madrid about thirty years later. Can this be the "unspeakable" Pi, once President of the Republic? Salmerón was different. "There had been something of vigour and honesty in the rule of Sr Salmerón, and the well-wishers of the distracted Peninsula were surprised and disappointed at the sudden announcement of his resignation from office."[2] Having praised his honesty, they immediately proceed to accuse him of duplicity. "It was probably from despair of his power to re-establish order that

[1] *Lecturas españolas* (Nelson edition), 223 ff.
[2] *Annual Register* (1873), 231.

Salmerón took this resolution, rather than from the pretext which he alleged. That pretext, a whimsical one enough under the circumstances, was his invincible objection to the infliction of capital punishment." When we have made the acquaintance of Sanz del Río, in the next chapter, we may conclude that his pupil Salmerón was honest enough in his objection; though it may well have been the impossible position in which he found himself that induced him to make capital punishment a question of resignation. The Cortes were determined that capital punishment should be restored to the Criminal Code; and to this Salmerón, as a humanitarian philosopher, could never agree.

Emilio Castelar came next. Though he had attended some of the lectures of Sanz del Río, the Krausist philosopher, he was not a Krausist himself, nor even a philosopher. He was more supple, more a man of action than either Pi y Margall or Salmerón, and he accepted the task of governing, although that meant the abandonment of all his principles for the good of the country. He had preached federalism for twenty years "with his own unexampled eloquence". Yet the moment he found himself at the helm (he governed the country from the 8th September, 1873, until the 2nd January, 1874) he had to recognize the fact that federalism for Spain was not practical politics. He had also to give up two other cherished convictions: his objections to capital punishment and to compulsory military service. Mr David Hannay, a good historian but a severe critic, who, as the son of a British consul at Barcelona, lived through many of the events which he describes and sometimes reveals the irritation of the moment rather than the serenity of the biographer, has paid a fine tribute to the character of Castelar, though he can never forgive him for being an orator.

The first effect of the responsibility of office on Don Emilio was to convince him that his theories could not even begin to be applied without plunging Spain into anarchy.... He used his power to avert the ruin of the country, but he had to work by using all the resources of a centralised administration, by permitting his officers to inflict that pain of death which he had wished to abolish, and by levying the most severe conscription ever raised in Spain, by using, in fact, the very things he had laboured to abolish.

"We must close for ever", he said, in his speech to the Cortes on the 2nd January, 1874, "the era of popular risings and military *pronunciamientos*." Even as he pronounced these words, the House was surrounded by the soldiers of General Pavía y Rodríguez de Albuquerque, and the republic was virtually at an end. Eleven months later, General Martínez Campos "pronounced" for Alfonso XII; and the monarchy was restored.

It might have been thought that the republicans, with such a record behind them, "must needs have been buried in ridicule", and that their leader would "have little to ask from his country-men except that they would be good enough to forget him". Castelar (says Mr Hannay) went back to the modest flat which he shared with his sister, and to his lectures, for he had never ceased to hold the chair of Philosophy of History in the University of Madrid. He found himself not only not ridiculous, but celebrated, and enjoying no small measure of respect.

That he earned respect and not ridicule is due to his success in convincing his countrymen of his honesty....There was novelty in the spectacle of a politician who really did seem to mean what he said....He had not always meant consistent things, but at the time of speaking, he was saying what he thought. So many politicians in Spain had begun no less humbly than Don Emilio, to end in the possession of fine houses, and fortunes of which the source was more or less mysterious, that he was thanked for returning to his quiet little home as poor as he left it....They may not have thought him much wiser, but they did think him honest, and that he had set a good example, which might be followed with advantage.

Castelar, no less than Pi y Margall and Salmerón, raised the level of what was expected from public men in Spain; and thus, though the Republic failed, the republicans of 1873 did their country no contemptible service.

III

SANZ DEL RÍO
the much-abused Philosopher

IN THE Spain of 1868 there was something beyond the mad-house of political and clerical intrigue, something beside the "sober citizens", the pawns in the game, who, however much and however excitedly they might discuss current events, considered those events merely as they might happen in the narrowest sense to affect themselves. That "something" was the group of philosophic radicals—the only men in Spain with whom a stranger from the north would have felt at home, or would feel at home now, if he could step into the Spanish past and listen to the talk of people in Madrid in 1868, for these men were to be the makers of modern Spain.

The centre of the group was a man belonging to an older generation, born in 1814. He came from Torrearévalo near Soria, one of the bleakest, if not most desolate spots in the whole of Spain. Scorching heat in summer, at an altitude of 3460 feet above the level of the sea; icy blasts in winter, from the snowy heights of Moncayo and Cebollera; a frozen, withering wind, in which only the strongest can survive. *Soria pura* (says the rhyme)

> Soria pura,
> cabeza de Estremadura.

Soria, more purely and uncompromisingly Castilian than any town in Castile, Old or New; Soria, "the head of Estremadura", head of the no-man's-land that once divided the Christians from the Moors. Yet Soria had its sculptors and architects; the sculptured portals of its Romanesque churches glow like a furnace in the afternoon sun; and the round-arched cloisters welcome you with a greater beauty and a greater peace than other Castilian cloisters. One of them (San Juan de Duero) has fallen—or can the bitter winds have blown it away? —leaving only its border of interlacing arches, like the skeleton of a leaf that has lain long in water. That is Soria.

This man who came from near Soria was the son of a farm labourer; yet he spoke and read several languages, spent two years at the University of Heidelberg, and was a professor in the University of Madrid until the government turned him out for not signing a certain declaration which was required of him—Professor Sanz del Río.

Julián Sanz del Río owed his education to an uncle, Don Fermín, a liberal-minded priest, who, on the death of the father in 1824, took the boy with him to Córdoba and put him into a seminary, where he learnt some little Latin and a smattering of scholastic philosophy. His schooling was continued at the College of the Sacro Monte at Granada—a grim barrack of a building, half-way up the mountain—and then at Toledo, where the kindly uncle had become a canon of the cathedral. In 1835 he was entered at the University of Granada, where he took the degrees of licentiate and doctor. At that time the ancient University of Alcalá de Henares, in spite of the beautiful buildings erected for it by Cardinal Ximénez, had just been moved to one of the least salubrious quarters of Madrid, and there Sanz del Río continued his studies in the law. In 1840 he was admitted to the degree of licentiate, after passing the examination with such distinction that the fees were remitted, a practice sometimes, but not often, followed in the case of a poor student.

He began the study of German. Who first introduced him to that study, and made him see that the drudgery of it was worth while? Two names have been suggested: Álvaro de Zafra and Ruperto Navarro Zamorano. Both were "in the law", affiliated to the *progresista* party, and reading all the new books which reached Spain from foreign countries. The latter, a friend and fellow-student of Sanz del Río, was interested in German legal philosophy—he afterwards published a translation of Ahrens' book on Natural Law; and it is probable that that was the book which gave this group of friends their ideas, and awoke in Sanz del Río the desire to learn German.[1]

[1] "En el centenario de Sanz del Río, por un discípulo" [Francisco Giner], *Boletín de la Institución Libre de Enseñanza*, 31 Aug. 1914, 225–31.

Heinrich Ahrens had been a pupil of the philosopher Karl Friedrich Krause (1781–1832). Sanz del Río seems to have heard of Krause and to have begun to study his system while he was still at Madrid. The side which most interested him was the philosophy of law, "the borderland (as Maitland put it) where ethical speculation marches with jurisprudence". In 1841 he proposed to the authorities the creation of a lectureship in the Philosophy of Law at the University of Madrid. At the time, no notice was taken. Two years later, a liberal Minister of Education, Pedro Gómez de la Serna, promised him a lectureship in a different subject, the History of Philosophy, if he would go abroad for two years and see how the subject was taught in foreign universities. So in 1843 he set out, "with such little knowledge as he had of the German language and German philosophy".[1] The government allowed him a grant towards his expenses,[2] and he also received assistance from his friend José de la Revilla, to whom he wrote long letters describing his progress.

Most of the Spaniards who had gone abroad before this time had done so for political reasons. They escaped across the Pyrenees into France, or they made their way to Gibraltar and so to England. There was a large colony of Spanish political refugees in London; the Lord Mayor had opened a fund for them, and was the recipient of laudatory sonnets and other marks of affection and esteem. Occasionally the wanderers went farther afield. A story of a Spaniard in Heidelberg—a real piece of Old Heidelberg gossip—is hinted and left half told in the memoirs of Professor Georg Weber the historian. In the thirties, at the time of the first Carlist war, a Spanish "statesman" named Tejada stayed for some time in Heidelberg. He had come on legal business concerned with Isabella's title to the throne which the Carlists disputed; and while Karl Röder and other famous jurists examined the material he brought and prepared a judgment in favour of Queen Isabella, Tejada

---

[1] *Cartas inéditas de Don Julián Sanz del Río publicadas por Don Manuel de la Revilla*, 9.

[2] *Ibid.*, 5.

amused himself with the ladies, among whom he was known as *der schöne Spanier*. Professor Weber is not very explicit; was it not a Madame Weber who was the object of passionate adoration on the part of another Heidelberg student of the time, Henri-Frédéric Amiel? The dovecotes of Heidelberg were considerably fluttered to hear that the mysterious Spanish stranger had been rewarded with the Grand Cross of Isabella the Catholic.[1]

Sanz del Río seems to have been the first Spaniard of modern times to go abroad purely for purposes of study, "the first Spanish professor pensioned in a foreign country since the time of Philip II", and the first of a long line of Spanish students who have done so since. The remarkable thing is that they have been nearly all of them either his pupils, or pupils of his pupils.

In Paris he attended the lectures of Victor Cousin, the philosopher of eclecticism. But they seem to have been wasted on him, and he makes a curious remark:

Every day I regret more and more the influence which French philosophy and French learning have exercised amongst us, for more than half a century. What has it brought us, except laziness in working for ourselves, false knowledge, and above all intellectual dishonesty and petulant egoism?[2]

He moved to Brussels, where Ahrens was able to instruct him further in the system of Krause; and there he writes, "In Brussels, and in my relations with M. Ahrens, I realized the difficulties of the (German) language, and particularly the philosophical language".[3] Ahrens advised him to go to Heidelberg, where the philosophy of Krause was at that time most seriously studied.

The University of Heidelberg was unlike anything he had known in Spain.

You must not think (he wrote to José de la Revilla) that a University means, or is, the same thing in Germany as in Spain. Our Universities are institutions where the teaching, formerly under the

---

[1] *Heidelberger Erinnerungen*, 238.   [2] *Cartas inéditas*, 20.
[3] *Ibid.* 10.

influence and even under the practical supervision of the Church, is now under that of the State. In Germany, the University, in its inner life and in the instruction which is given, is totally independent of both Church and State; and in order that it may be true knowledge that is taught there, neither State nor Church has legal power to intervene in its affairs.[1]

In order to see the full force of this, it should be remembered that in France, Italy and Spain the universities are departments of the State; degrees are conferred in the name of the State, and the possession of a State degree is necessary before a man or woman may practise any of the learned professions. In Germany the universities are official establishments, but possess a wide measure of autonomy. They provide the training and confer the degrees which certify it; but the examinations for the learned professions are conducted by the State. In England, as we know, the State abstains from direct intervention, although when it provides a government grant, it imposes certain conditions.

At Heidelberg Sanz del Río heard the lectures of some of the most celebrated philosophers and jurists of the day. There was Karl Röder (1806–79), a pupil of Krause, who did much valuable work for prison reform; Theodor Schliephake, author of an introduction to the systems of philosophy and a large *History of Nassau*; Hermann von Leonhardi (1809–75) who arranged an International Congress of Philosophy at Prague in 1868, and who has a permanent place in the history of German education. Sanz del Río lodged in the house of Professor Georg Weber himself, who was the author of a history of the Reformation in England, and a *History of the World* which was translated into Spanish by Sanz del Río, and which, by 1929, had reached its twenty-fourth German edition. Sanz del Río is not mentioned in any of the professor's memoirs; but he made friends with Georg Gervinus (1805–71), the commentator of Shakespeare and historian of German poetry; and he was on terms of intimacy with old Friedrich Schlosser, the

[1] *Cartas inéditas*, 21.

historian of the eighteenth century, who had been born as long ago as 1776.

One of Sanz del Río's contemporaries at Heidelberg was Henri-Frédéric Amiel. They may even have lived in the same house—the house of the Madame Weber with whom Amiel began one of his first and most romantic love-affairs. Both Amiel and Sanz del Río preserved throughout their lives a memory of their student friendship, and it was made the stronger by their devotion to the same philosophical ideas.[1] They were both admirers of Krause, and Amiel's editors admit that Krause must be given a prominent place in his philosophical training. In Heidelberg, the reading of this philosopher exercised an extraordinary attraction for him; while afterwards, in Berlin, it became one of his favourite studies. "The man", he says in one of the fragments of his diary recently published, "who most seems to me to have realized my type of mind is Krause; for in him, idea, beauty and love are in a balanced harmony, co-ordinated but not absorbed by the pure intelligence."[2] Krause had been dead a dozen years when Amiel and Sanz del Río were students at Heidelberg; but he exercised a profound influence over the young Swiss student, although that influence was not so great on Amiel as it was on Sanz del Río, through whom he contributed more than any other thinker to the transformation of the Spanish mind. The two did not correspond much in after years; only one letter from Amiel has been found among the papers of Sanz del Río—a letter written on the occasion of the revolution of 1868, and pointing out how useless a Spanish revolution would be if it did not root out the theocratic bias from Spanish life. Clericalism (Amiel wrote) had always been the great obstacle to Spanish progress.[3]

When the two years at Heidelberg were over, Sanz del Río returned to Spain and was duly appointed to his lectureship; but to the surprise of his friends he renounced the post, saying that he did not consider himself sufficiently prepared to occupy

[1] Posada, "Krause, Amiel, Sanz del Río", *Boletín* (1930), 847.
[2] Marañon, *Amiel: un estudio sobre la timidez*, 16.
[3] Llopis, *Crisol*, 15 July, 1931.

it. His uncle was dead, he had inherited some little property, and he retired to Illescas with his two sisters, to read and meditate and go for long country walks.

Illescas is a gaunt, Castilian country town half-way between Madrid and Toledo, where the shields of hidalgo families slowly crumble to dust over the doors of the houses, and the church tower, built by Muslim bricklayers for Christian worshippers, has row upon row of little Moorish windows, looking inwards—on to nothing. But there is something else in Illescas, something symbolical of a scholar's retreat. In the church of a charity hospital founded by Cardinal Ximénez is a painting by El Greco, a magnificent portrait of a learned man: San Ildefonso, Archbishop of Toledo. Galdós was fortunate as an author, in being able to hear the actual voice of one of his own characters in fiction, as we have seen in Chapter 1. San Ildefonso was even more fortunate; for the subject of his book appeared to him in a vision as he was writing. In the picture, the book is still being written, and the saint (muffled up, as he seems, in full canonicals) is keeping the place with his left hand, while he raises the right with a grey quill pen between his fingers. He has not yet seen the vision of the Virgin Mary, appearing in front of a rich piece of silk brocade, and is anxiously considering the *mot juste*. The sober luxury of that room is no less attractive than the man in it. The armchair with bronze ornaments and red silk tassels; the crimson velvet tablecloth, with a long fringe, golden clasps at the corners and trimmings of gold lace; the Spanish china ink-pots and the silver sand-box. "He is the prototype of our humanist devotional writers of the sixteenth century. They must have looked like that, and like that they must have meditated as they wrote their books."[1]

Sanz del Río lived at Illescas for nine years, from 1845 until 1854. It has been stated, on insufficient evidence, that he went back to Germany; actually he seems to have lived quietly in the country town, his room covered with thick mats of esparto grass and having a single window, high up in the wall and only reached by a ladder. On that ladder he often used to sit, "taking

[1] Cossío, *El Greco*, I, 313–14.

the sun"; winters are severe in the province of Toledo. Once a month he went to Madrid, to talk about philosophy with a few friends at the house of Simón Santos Lerín—who was afterwards to become a famous lawyer. The house was at the corner of the Calle de la Luna and the Calle de Panaderas (the junction of Moon Street and Baker Street) in that quarter of old Madrid which just escaped the destruction caused by the Gran Vía, between the university and the Calle del Desengaño, the "Street of Disillusion", famous for its second-hand bookshops. These meetings led to the formation of a "philosophical circle", which had many years of fruitful existence.

At last, in 1853, he applied to be readmitted to the university, "believing himself by that time more competent to occupy a professorial chair"; and he sent in a number of philosophical works which had occupied him at Illescas, together with Spanish translations, enlarged with special chapters on Spain, of books by some of his German friends.[1]

The revolution of 1854 (which caused far more bloodshed than that which dethroned Isabella in 1868) interrupted the projects for printing Sanz del Río's works; but he was duly elected to a professorship (that of the History of Philosophy) and at once his lectures were crowded, not only by undergraduates but by men of mature age, and politicians. A group was quickly formed to spread the teaching of the new master, Krause; everyone who wanted to be in touch with modern ideas, or who was interested in German thought, joined the school of Sanz del Río.

Who was Krause, and what was his system? Many professed students of philosophy might be puzzled for an answer. "Krause?" a young German asked in surprise, a man whose father and grandfather had both been connected with the

---

[1] Sketches of an *Analytical Metaphysics*, and a *Theory of the Sensations*; translations of Weber's *Universal History*, amplified with introduction, notes and a special supplement on Spain (vol. 1, privately printed), and of Ahrens' *Psychology*; a new and revised edition in Spanish of Krause's *Ideal of Humanity*, and a History of German literature founded on Gervinus and Weber, with comparative notes on the literature of Spain.

University of Heidelberg, once supposed to be the stronghold
of the Krausist philosophy. "Krause? That's no philosopher!
That's a barber or a waiter! It's impossible that there should be
a philosopher called Krause!" Yet Krause the philosopher did
definitely exist, and he was neither a barber nor a waiter.

Karl Christian Friedrich Krause was born at Eisenberg, near
Jena, in 1781. He studied at that university with Hegel and
Fichte, and then removed to Dresden where lack of pupils in
philosophy compelled him to give lessons in music. Several of
his books deal with musical subjects, and one of them, originally
published about 1827, was thought worthy of a new edition in
1911. Krause seems to have wandered disconsolately from one
university to another in the hope of a professorship; but the
chair was never forthcoming and he died in Munich in comparative obscurity in 1832. It was unfortunate for Krause that
he was a contemporary of both Fichte and Hegel, for his work,
important as it was, was completely overshadowed by theirs.
His books are difficult reading, even for Germans; his style is
confused, and he is constantly inventing new words, or using
familiar words in unfamiliar ways. His special doctrine is
termed "panentheism" (*Allingottlehre*), because it asserts that
God, as the Absolute Being, "that which does not include
contradiction", has the whole world within Himself, without,
however, being exhausted in the world.[1] Nature and Spirit are
(he affirmed) the real and the ideal; in the former predominates
the character of "wholeness" (*Ganzheit*); in the latter, that of
"selfhood" (*Selbstheit*). God is the principle common to both.
Humanity unites in itself the higher natural organism, the
human body, and the rational consciousness of self (*Selbst-
bewusstsein*). Terrestrial humanity is only a small part of universal
humanity, which constitutes the Divine Kingdom.[2]

This philosophic doctrine became of special significance for
the philosophy of law, owing to the prominence given to the
conception of humanity as forming an organic whole made in

---

[1] Höffding, *History of Modern Philosophy* (1900), II, 268.
[2] Falckenberg, *La Filosofía alemana desde Kant...traducido y adicionado por
F. Giner*, 78–81.

the image of the Divine or Primal Being, and to the view that law is the form in which the life of this whole is developed.[1] Law (it is claimed) should not be limited merely to the external conditions of the use of liberty, but should order the whole life of humanity in such a way that each of its members may approach without let or hindrance the ultimate goal of his moral perfection. The same is true for associations—the family, partnership, races, peoples, societies—as it is for individuals.[2]

"The term panentheism," Eucken remarks, "first employed by Krause, best expresses the religious attitude of the German classical epoch. Every form of creation appeared to be comprehended in one being, and to be founded in divine wisdom— a wisdom operating everywhere, not from without, but as an emanation of the inmost being of every form of creation; and this wisdom found its fullest expression in the free and rational human organism, *i.e.* in man."[3] Eucken again must have had Krause in mind when he wrote: "All that this cultured circle does is inspired by a courageous and joyful outlook on the world and on life. Not that there is any subscribing to a comfortable optimism, which smooths away all problems from the outset. The problems are deeply realised and life is seen to be full of difficult tasks. The optimism lies in this, that our mental force is deemed equal to the tasks and the shock of collision is felt as taxing our capacity to the utmost, but not as barring or stultifying our effort. It is impossible to place any high value on mental work, unless we believe that it has a cosmic setting, and that behind human undertakings there is the support of a Divine Power. Thus religious conviction is looked upon with no disfavour, but it is rather an admission of infinity into man's finite life, an acknowledgement of an unseen order of things, than a movement towards a new world not to be gained save through shock and rebellion."[4]

[1] Höffding, *loc. cit.*
[2] Vorländer, *History of Philosophy*, II, cap. xvi, § 52 (4).
[3] Eucken, *Collected Essays* (1914), 462.
[4] Eucken, *The Problem of Human Life* (1914), 462. See also his *Festrede* delivered on the centenary of Krause's birth, *Zur Erinnerung an K. Ch. F. Krause* (Leipzig, 1881).

In Spain, Krausism represents more than merely a philosophical system, with its principles, its problems and its solutions. It was a combination of the different forms of rationalist thought in politics, religion and philosophy, and stood in opposition to the scholastic tradition. If it seemed unconvincing to thinkers temperamentally inclined to accept rather than to question, it was rank heresy to those who had been taught to accept without thinking or questioning at all. Moreover, Sanz del Río offended the more orthodox minds by his method of teaching—by his preference for private tuition and for a small class of students who already knew something of the subject, to a large, showy public lecture in which there was an impassable barrier between the lecturer and his audience. He did not expound philosophical principles in the formal, accepted manner. Like Kant (he said) he did not teach men philosophy, but to be philosophers. His lectures, and particularly his inaugural lecture at the beginning of the academic year,[1] were inclined to "degenerate" into an informal eulogy of the moral effects of philosophy on the character and an exhortation to young men to study it as law and self-discipline.

That might be all very well in England; but in a Latin, Catholic country, it would not do. Its tone (said his enemies) was half sentimental, half Stoic; everything he said tended to inculcate independence of thought and "the damnable morality of Kantian ethics", which he held to supersede those ethical systems deriving their force from a special revelation. Belief in God (so Kant taught) sprang from morality; not morality from belief in God. The moral law was something original and independent; religion came afterwards, the recognition of our duties as divine precepts. The moral law did not bind us because God required obedience; it was necessary to establish the moral or rational character of a precept, before attributing to it a divine origin. Religion had no other meaning than to fortify the influence of the moral law by means of the idea of the majesty of the Divine Legislator. The "Son of God" was to be

[1] The inaugural lecture for the academic year 1857–8, on the mission of a university, is printed by Zozaya, *Biblioteca económica filosófica*, vol. IX.

understood as the idea of perfect man. Faith in Him did not mean the belief that Christ was the Son of God, but the receiving by our will of the idea of moral perfection. That was the philosophical meaning of the idea of the *Logos*. That was roughly the Kantian position, as expounded by Sanz del Río, and more particularly by his pupil Giner de los Ríos.[1] Kant (unsound though his theology might be) was more or less intelligible, even to those who had been trained in a seminary. But as for Sanz del Río, not even Menéndez y Pelayo could make out what *he* meant, as the quotations he gave (as specimens of "Krausist" style) abundantly prove. Menéndez y Pelayo, librarian of the Biblioteca Nacional, was the great "polygraph" of Restoration Spain, who wrote voluminously and with immense learning on literature, philosophy, heresy, and a variety of other subjects; but the philosophy of Krause—and German philosophy in general—was antipathetic to his narrow scholastic nature. Even the Second Part of Goethe's *Faust* could be dismissed with the remark: "What have I to do with the amours of a German professor with Helen of Troy?" While as to the philosophy of Sanz del Río and the Spanish Krausists, it was sheer hypocrisy! *Socrates damnatus est quia*—well, we all know why *that* was! Sanz del Río was condemned because, using the principles of Krause as an instrument, he invited his hearers to think for themselves. A certain Manuel Ortí y Lara heard one lecture, and considered throne and altar to be in such danger that he spent the rest of his life in attacking Sanz del Río and the theories of Krause. He even learned German for that purpose. There was something revolting in those doctrines, something which came into violent collision with "feelings which are co-substantial with the history of our Spanish philosophical ideas". Menéndez y Pelayo, in the elegant controversial manner of which he was so great a master, referred to the Krausian doctrines of Sanz del Río as an Eleusinian mystery concealed by gibberish; a fetid skeleton with whose sterile caresses we have been soliciting and exciting the passions of the youth of Spain for so many years.[2]

---

[1] In his Spanish edition of Falckenberg.   [2] *Heterodoxos españoles*, III.

The ideas of Sanz del Río would not have seemed strange in the north of Europe or America. His public lecture at the beginning of the academic year, which so upset the egregious Ortí y Lara, was not unlike many such inaugural lectures which have been given at centres of learning in England; it might be compared to one of the "College Addresses" delivered by Sir Hubert Parry at the Royal College of Music. But such things seemed unusual, and therefore immoral, from the point of view of traditional Spanish philosophy, as expounded by Father Balmes.

"Spanish philosophy? (an English or German student might remark) I didn't know there was any"; and even in Spain, Balmes himself (who was at least a respectable thinker) was described not long ago as being "no philosopher, but a liberal priest; an admirable journalistic pen, with a theology to defend".[1] Menéndez y Pelayo also had a theology to defend; but he spoke more truly than he knew, when he wrote:

> It is a shameful thing for Spain that when the whole civilized world, without distinction of believers and unbelievers, rocks with Homeric laughter over such visions—only worthy of Don Quixote in the Cave of Montesinos—a horde of sectarian fanatics...has succeeded in atrophying the understanding of a whole generation, loading it with the bonds of slavery and cutting it off from the rest of the world, spreading over our university teaching a darkness thicker than that of the Cimmerian plains.[2]

The famous "polygraph" meant this to apply to Sanz del Río and the "Krausists"; but we see now where the cap really fits.

Sanz del Río and his followers became something more than a school. They stood by one another in difficulty and persecution; and what they thought, they tried to bring down to practical life. They paid attention to elementary education, and endeavoured to make the Master's views penetrate even to the lowest grades of primary instruction. In 1862 Sanz del Río published a "programme" of education in psychology, logic and ethics, consisting of only twenty-nine pages; and his example

---

[1] *Gaceta Literaria*, 1 April, 1929.   [2] *Heterodoxos*, III, 731–2.

was followed by others among his pupils, who have tried (then and since) to say what was in their minds in the fewest possible words. This was particularly galling to Menéndez y Pelayo, in the spacious times of the restoration. For so voluminous a writer, never content with less than three volumes, it was exasperating to find that there were people who could say everything they had to say, and express themselves clearly, in a single leaflet.

In addition to his lectures at the university, Sanz del Río founded the "Philosophical Circle", to which reference has already been made, where men might meet to discuss philosophical problems. First it met in the professor's house, and then moved to larger quarters elsewhere. Besides Sanz del Río himself, the learned and virtuous master Fernando de Castro could be heard there, and above all Emilio Castelar, the greatest orator of the century.

Castelar has already been referred to in the last chapter. Fernando de Castro deserves something more than passing notice. He was born at Sahagún, in the north, a grim, gaunt town in the province of León, overshadowed by a heavy brick tower and the ruins of a vast abbey where early kings of León retired to end their days as monks. Fernando de Castro was educated for the priesthood, but decided to enter a religious order. He chose the Franciscan; and being placed in charge of the infirmary, "sought out and collected aromatic herbs with which to wash the feet of monks who should stop there on their way". From the first he gave signs of a humility and patience that were truly evangelical; but a certain spiritual unrest took possession of him; he left the monastery (possibly on account of the exclaustration of the religious orders in 1835) and passed to the secular religious life. He joined the seminary at León, where he became Vice-Rector, and founded the interesting and valuable Provincial Library. Then he was transferred to Madrid, having won by competitive examination a teaching post in the Institución de San Isidro. A university appointment followed, and the nomination as honorary chaplain to the Queen. His sermons were considered rather extraordinary; they were not

pleasing to court and Catholic circles. He read foreign books—
the writings of one Newman, for instance, an Englishman,
whom no one in Spain had ever heard of. He was elected a
member of the Academy of History; but his inaugural discourse, his *discurso de entrada*, on the history of the Church in
Spain, was too puzzling to be orthodox. It drew a gently
critical but appreciative reply from Francisco Giner; and
orthodox circles then became aware that Fernando de Castro
was in relation with those dangerous men who read German and
studied German philosophy—above all with the eccentric
Professor Sanz del Río himself.

The rest of the acts of Fernando de Castro can only be
summarized here. He made a version of *Don Quixote* especially for children; he interested himself in the education of
women. In February, 1869, "the learned and virtuous master"
inaugurated a course of Sunday lectures on women's education
and himself delivered a discourse which was described at the
time as most notable. Its candid, outworn sentiments come to
us to-day like a breath from another world, as from a mahogany
cabinet of the period of Queen Isabella, filled with fans, and
daguerreotypes, and locks of hair. But it is, at any rate, an
advance upon *The Perfect Wife* written in the sixteenth century
by another austere ecclesiastic, whose knowledge of women was
derived partly from Santa Teresa and partly from *The Song of
Songs*, from the most divinely human (it might be said) to the
most humanly divine—the perfect poet, Luis de León. For
Fernando de Castro, woman was no longer a chattel; she was an
inspiration. But we will leave the fragile petals of his discourse
behind the glass door of the Isabelline cabinet.

Ladies (he concluded), it is essential that you raise the level of your
education, if you would achieve the ends of your desire. When you
have done that, you will influence men to be worth something, and
be something, in the life and history of their time; something in the
religion, something in the politics of your country, something in the
other spheres and objects of existence. But take care! Do not try to
impose upon them any of your own views on religion, or politics, or
any other subject. Your destiny as wives and mothers is to advise and

to influence; not on any account to rule. The moment you try to do that, to exercise pressure on a man, trusting to the ascendancy and power over him given by your tears or your weakness, you commit the most grave and unpardonable fault. With my hand on my conscience I assure you that there is no right, divine or human, which obliges you to impose anything on a man, even in the matter of religion.[1]

Dear innocent Don Fernando! A woman not to influence a man in the matter of religion? No wonder the Spanish Church fell foul of him, for he was depriving it of one of its most subtle and effective instruments. Yet he persisted in his error. He founded a Ladies' Athenaeum, a school for teachers, and (in 1873) an Association for Women's Education which still exists. He died in 1874, having devoted his latest energies to the abolition of slavery in Cuba.

The ladies whom he sought to educate were puzzled, fluttered. The austere intellectual, to whom learning seemed to offer so vast a firmament for the flight of the spirit, had fallen into the misfortune of attempting to analyse dogma, and was sinking into the pit of doubt. Though gifted by God with an upright and impartial spirit, he had not succeeded in finding light or consolation to bring him to tranquillity; neither in the *Confessions* of St Augustine, nor in the *Imitation of Christ* nor in the *Spiritual Combat* of Scaramelli, nor in the *Introduction à la vie dévote* of St Francis de Sales. So he had withdrawn from the Church of Rome, though he declared in his will that he had always observed the vows which he had taken on being ordained priest. And this man was the founder of the School for Teachers, and the Association for the Education of Women, the cornerstone of feminism in Spain in the nineteenth century! How inscrutable are the ways of Providence![2]

The apostolic founder of the Association for the Education of Women does indeed represent a beginning of the new spirit in the Spanish universities, one that was apparently extinguished at the restoration of 1875, but which continued to glow un-

[1] Aguilera y Arjona, 356–7.
[2] Concepción Sáiz, *La Revolución de 68 y la cultura feminina*, 31.

obtrusively until the foundation of the residential university college for women (Residencia de Señoritas) in 1915.

With members such as Fernando de Castro and Sanz del Río, the Philosophical Circle was naturally regarded by clericals as a centre of heretical propaganda, and by conservatives as a focus of revolution. They were quite right. The Circle included the best Spanish brains of the time, both in learning and politics. The doctrines of Sanz del Río were gradually converted into radical propaganda, a transformation which was not unnatural, considering the backwardness, both political and social, of Spain at that time. The suspicions of the authorities were aroused. The inaugural lecture of 1857 had "created an atmosphere unfavourable to the professor". In 1865 he was accused—by those who had half read him, or had only heard about his theories from others who had half read him—of "pantheism" (perhaps a confusion with the "panentheism" of Krause) and of corrupting healthy ideas. One of his works achieved the distinction of being put on the *Index*. Newspapers demanded his expulsion from the university. Questions were asked in the Cortes. The government gave way. A reactionary minister, the Marqués de Orovio, seized his opportunity. In 1867 he required all professors to sign an extravagantly worded declaration of faith—religious, political and dynastic, as a manifesto of "adhesion" to the Queen who had been the object of certain attacks in the foreign press. Sanz del Río refused to sign, justifying himself by the laws then in force; and like Fernando de Castro, Francisco Giner, Nicolás Salmerón and other reformers—makers of modern Spain—was deprived of his professorial chair. Sanz del Río received a message of sympathy from the University of Heidelberg signed by sixty-three professors and doctors, including names such as Helmholtz, Zeller, Bluntschli, Wundt, Eucken, Schlosser, Bunsen, men of international reputation, Catholics, Protestants and Free-thinkers; while another protest was received from the International Philosophical Congress assembled at Prague.[1]

[1] The protests, and Sanz del Río's reply, are printed in *Boletín-Revista de la Universidad de Madrid*, 1, nos. 5, 6 (March, 1869).

The provisional government of 1868 restored Sanz del Río to his chair; he was nominated Rector (or, as we should say, Vice-Chancellor) of the university; but he declined the honour, and in the year after, he died at the early age of 52, leaving his books to the university, and enough money to found a new lecture-ship in the faculty of philosophy.

Sanz del Río's importance does not rest only on his philosophical writings, numerous as they are both in print and in manuscript. His greatest work was accomplished as a teacher; and his teaching renewed the whole philosophical, moral and intellectual outlook of Spain.

The true signal and proof of his passage through the world of the national Spanish spirit lies in the difference—as small or as great as you like to make it—between the intellectual Spain of 1868 and the Spain before that. The difference is chiefly due to Sanz del Río. The ten years from 1860 to 1870—if so arbitrary limits can be fixed—are an awakening from the intellectual torpor of former days to the murmur of modern European thought and to the new problems and new positions of philosophy.[1]

The philosophy of Sanz del Río possesses a deeply ingrained moral and practical tendency, and this enables us to understand its powerful influence on Spanish life. This is the philosopher's most personal note, since the content of his thought is generally confined to the ideas expounded by Krause. It culminates in a passion for the organization of human activities, and therefore encourages a spirit of co-operation and universal harmony. "Philosophy (said the late J. V. Viqueira) is the great educator of humanity...always presenting herself anew in every great crisis. Against the false doctrine of the Sophists arose Socrates as representing true philosophy, against the frivolity of the eighteenth century stood Kant with his moral vigour; and against the threat to the basis of individual liberty and the personal merit of virtue, came Krause enjoining us to do good for the sake of good as a divine precept."[2]

[1] "En el centenario de Sanz del Río", *Boletín*, 31 Aug. 1914.

[2] J. V. Viqueira, app. to Spanish trans. of Vorländer's *History of Philosophy*, II, 448.

Philosophy diverts man from the world of sense to the world of spirit, as to a central oasis of serenity in which he may recruit his tired forces, and test his means of action by adjusting them to historical necessities, and may lift up his eyes to contemplate the ends of existence, obscured and well-nigh forgotten under the stress of private and immediate necessities.[1]

From his philosophy Sanz del Río hoped to achieve the spiritual redemption of Spain. "To that he dedicated his whole life, in silent and modest heroism to preach, teach and live it." The sense which penetrates his work is an intimately religious sense; "for (as he said) every useful work which sheds light or brings good in its train is, in the highest sense and in its ultimate consequences, a religious work". His religion, however, was in no sense confessional or dogmatic; it might almost be reduced "to a universal sense of life", to a conviction that the designs of providence are realized in the world.

We must remember that we are in the 'sixties of the last century, in a country far from the centres of philosophic thought and scientific inquiry, or we shall find it difficult to understand how fertile these ideas have been, or realize that such ideas—which at that time were an unheard-of novelty in Spain and seemed to possess a decidedly revolutionary character—could have attracted so large a number of disciples. Yet the work of Sanz del Río had enormous importance for Spain, and constituted, either directly by his disciples or indirectly by arousing discussion, a renaissance of philosophic studies and of scientific activity, which in their turn were translated into a definite raising of the moral and cultural level. Sanz del Río attracted all the better minds to philosophy, and opened the eyes of Spain to the intellectual life of Europe.[2] For the first time Spanish interest was turned to German philosophy, and Sanz del Río was the first Spanish thinker whose knowledge of the German language enabled him to get directly in touch with German minds.

Sanz del Río was not an original thinker. His system (as we

[1] Sanz del Río, in *Bibl. Econ. Fil.* IX, I.
[2] Viqueira, *History of Philosophy*, II, 449.

saw) was adapted from Krause. He was above all a teacher who understood philosophy in the Socratic manner, as a method and as an instrument of personal perfection. He did not discover any new points of view; but he had a vocation for teaching, and into that he put his whole life and soul. His contemporaries —those of them who knew English—said of him what Pope said of Mr Gay:

In wit, a man; simplicity, a child.

To-day the Krausist philosophy has disappeared. There is probably not a single Krausist in Germany; while in Spain, the present generation regard Krausism as something monstrous; contemporary philosophy (they say) has got far away from those placid waters. Yet the Spanish Krausists were important, not because they were Krausists, but because they were philosophers, because their intellectual attitude was adequate to the occasion, and was a correct attitude for the philosophical spirit to take up. "The instrument, the Krausian system, was of less importance. What was valuable in it was the intellectual integrity with which the instrument was used. Intellectual integrity means knowledge, it means the absence of blindness and of mists, both in speaking and writing; and to-day the higher culture of Spain, and the organisms, institutions and persons which represent it, descend by easily identified paths from that group which was once a non-conforming minority."[1]

[1] *Gaceta Literaria*, 1 April, 1929.

IV

DON FRANCISCO GINER (I)
A Society of Friends

AMONG the younger generation of those who attended the lectures of Sanz del Río was a student from the south of Spain, with "eyes that went through you like arrows",[1] and the remains of a mop of romantic black hair—Francisco Giner. Don Francisco Giner de los Ríos was born at Ronda, his mother's country, in 1839. In that wild hill-town there is a great gorge, dividing the medieval Muslim quarter, with its planless, winding streets and stout walnut doors, from the neo-classic Christian settlement of well-planned blocks of houses with heavy green iron gratings over the windows. The gorge is crossed by a bridge, 400 feet high (even the architect turned giddy and fell into the abyss); near that, in the old town, is a house with an inscription commemorating the birth of Don Francisco Giner. The house is modern; it is not the building in which Don Francisco was born; but beside it is an older, lower house, with wrought iron balconies and a spacious doorway, which enables us to see what the other house must have been like a hundred years ago, when Don Francisco was born there.[2]

The population of Ronda in those days (according to Richard Ford, who visited it between 1830 and 1834) consisted chiefly of "bold, brave, fresh-complexioned mountaineers, smugglers and bull-fighters"; the damsels, "unlike those of tawny Andalucia", were as fresh and ruddy as the pippins. True believers, who wished to shorten the pangs of purgatory, could do much in a month at Ronda; in the Church of the Socorro they might obtain a million days' indulgence, while the longevity of Ronda was expressed in the proverb: *En Ronda los hombres a ochenta son pollones*, in Ronda the men of eighty are still chickens. There were a few well-to-do families, and

---

[1] *Ojos de agresiva saeta.*
[2] Luis Bello, *Viaje por las escuelas de España*, II, 94.

they led a sociable life, especially in summer when other families came up from Seville and Málaga. The Giners, though belonging to Vélez Málaga, had come originally from the east coast, Valencia; the name "Giner" is said to be a form of the Latin *Januarius*. In *The Qâdîs of Córdoba*, an Arabic book written in Spain in the tenth century, there is a story of a man of the same name (here spelt *Yanair*) who had so great a reputation for honesty that his services were frequently required in the law-courts as a witness. On one occasion the conduct of a *qâdî*, or magistrate, was being investigated, and Yanair was called to give evidence. He spoke no Arabic (in spite of being a devout Muslim), and his evidence was given in the primitive Latin-Spanish dialect which Muslims called "the outlandish language". "No, I do not know him," Yanair answered, "but I have heard tell of him that he is a little... ", and he used a diminutive of the word in the outlandish language. That language and the curiously sounding words used by the natives of Spain, were a perpetual source of amusement to the Arabic-speaking rulers; even the Emir of Córdoba, Prince of Believers, was fond of asking his courtiers what certain things, not always mentioned in polite Arabic speech, were called in "Latin". Yanair's diminutive was too good to be lost; it was at once passed on, and the Emir exclaimed: "Verily such a word could not have come from such a man, unless it were true!" and he dismissed the *qâdî* forthwith.

On his mother's side Giner de los Ríos was Andaluz. The most distinguished member of the family was Antonio de los Ríos Rosas, a politician whom even a severe foreign critic could describe as "the soul of honour". He was a moderate liberal and an academician, "an iron-grey man of middle age, an energetic and effective speaker". On one occasion he was understood to say in the Cortes that he regarded the Spanish army as "a horde of assassins". Asked by the Speaker whether he were prepared to put that statement in writing, he replied: "I would have it carved in stone if I could". He defended the principle of monarchy, but not the dynasty of the Bourbons; and although he died in 1873 before "the conspiracy of

Saguntum" restored the monarchy in the person of Alfonso XII, his funeral—he was buried in the National Pantheon of St Francis the Great—was attended by the President and all the republican leaders. He had, in fact, been in touch with all the republican groups, his intermediary being that scapegrace nephew of his, Francisco Giner, who in other respects was throwing away all the chances of a great political career which his own talents and his uncle's influence had opened to him.

The father of Francisco Giner had been an official of the Revenue Department, holding appointments in various towns in Spain: his son's early schooling therefore was acquired at different places. At Granada, one of his earliest teachers was Don José Aguilera, whose family still maintains its connection with education. This Don José often attended school in the uniform of the National Militia; on coming into the room he would unbuckle his sword and lay it beside him on the table.[1] Don Francisco's university studies began at Barcelona and ended at Granada where he took his degree in law, carrying away with him a supreme contempt for the way in which that subject was taught and the students' time wasted. Two teachers, however, left upon him a lasting impression. One of these was Francisco Javier Llorens, the Catalan philosopher, of whose instruction in Barcelona Giner never spoke without emotion. Llorens, he used to say, was the strongest influence of those early years—a truly educative influence, not so much in what he taught as in the severe discipline of his mind and the lofty idealism of his life.[2]

"What a man! What a complete man!" he would exclaim. Indeed Llorens seems to have had a fair share of those little eccentricities and foibles which make a schoolmaster remembered and bring back fragments of a lesson long afterwards. His honesty and his sense of citizenship reached such a pitch as to be almost incredible. In that troubled epoch of *pronunciamientos* and civil wars, Llorens, in his frequent journeys to and

[1] Luis Bello, *Viaje por las escuelas de España*, II, 94.
[2] F. Giner, *Obras completas*, vol. III, introduction by Manuel B. Cossío, p. xvii.

from Barcelona, would often be asked to carry messages between his friends. "Now Don Javier, you will be so kind as to give this letter to So-and-so, won't you?" And Don Javier would accept it with all possible amiability. But afterwards he would go into a tobacconist's, buy one of the old red four-*cuarto* stamps with the head of Isabella II, and stick it on the letter so as not to defraud the government, although he duly delivered the letter with his own hands. As a teacher he was most remarkable for his extremely individual manner of expression, and his way of questioning his pupils. When they were new and unknown to him, he had "an especially graceful way of sounding them, so as to give himself an idea of what each one could do". He was a man whose heart was in his work, a teacher with the true vocation for teaching.[1] Don Francisco relates that Llorens, when he heard any of his colleagues complain of the exiguous stipend assigned to them by the government, would reply:

Well, I, for my part, regard the question from another point of view; and I think myself a lucky man with much to be thankful for. How can it seem little to me, the amount I receive for my professorship, when I would have given all that I possess to hold it! Providence has permitted me to fulfil the highest aspiration of my life.[2]

At Granada, again, there was one teacher who interested Don Francisco, besides the "Inspector" of the College of Santiago where he was a boarder, José Fernández Jiménez, "a supreme example of the Spanish race in the tragic contrast between the abundance of his natural gifts and the small harvest of ripened fruits".[3] That teacher was Francisco Fernández y González. Though he held the chair of general and Spanish literature, he was by choice an orientalist, being the translator of Ibn 'Adhâri's Arabic history of "al-Andalus" (*i.e.* Moorish Spain), an authority on the social conditions of the Moors who came under Christian dominion, the juristic institutions of the Israelites in the different states of the Peninsula, and the in-

[1] Carreras i Artau, *Introducció a la història del pensament filosòfic a Catalunya*, 231.
[2] "Spencer y las buenas maneras", in Giner's *Obras completas*, VII, 173–4.
[3] *Obras completas*, III, xvii.

fluence of Oriental languages and literatures on the cultures of
Spain and Portugal; he once gave a famous lecture at the Ateneo
in Madrid on the languages spoken by the natives of North and
Central America. Fernández y González did not make Giner
into an orientalist, but he made him learn German—a language
which must be as difficult for a Spaniard as Arabic is for an
Englishman; he introduced him to German literature, and,
what was more important, to German philosophy.

About this time, too, someone in Granada made him acquainted with classical music, and above all with the music of
Mozart. He learnt to play the pianoforte a little, had a good
musical memory, and played some of Mozart's Sonatas "with
ease and refinement". He could not bear Chopin; although
when he played a slow movement by Mozart he made it sound
more like Chopin than he knew, bringing out its singing
qualities and its romantic reminiscences of great opera singers of
the past. One day, a pupil, not knowing his aversion to Chopin's
music, played one of the Mazurkas in Don Francisco's presence.
When he had finished, Don Francisco went to the pianoforte
and extemporized an ingenious parody of Chopin's style. He
sometimes extemporized in a more serious vein. This practical
knowledge of music, small though it may have been, brought
serenity to his soul and gave weight to his words when, later in
life, he came to speak of musical education.

In 1862 Francisco Giner was still at Granada, paying little
attention to the regular university courses but reading widely
for himself. His chief interest was already in philosophy; Kant,
Hegel, Ahrens and Krause. His desultory reading at that time
was already varied and copious, as it continued to be in later life.
He used afterwards to recommend his pupils never to let a day
pass without looking at some review or newspaper in a foreign
language, and he would tell them how much he had learnt from
the *Revue des Deux Mondes* during his student days at Granada.

He also helped, to the extent of almost being assistant editor,
in a review published at Granada, the *Revista Meridional*,
founded in 1862 by a regional poet, Trinidad de Rojas. The
Revista Meridional was "one of those old-fashioned provincial

publications, meagre in appearance and badly produced, where the reader who many years afterwards turns the yellowing pages with his heart still alive within him, will quickly perceive the intensely moving power of the humble things of long ago ". And, if he is Spanish, "it will not be surprising if they engender in his mind a feeling of melancholy or even of bitterness at the thought of how much Spain has lost in the spiritual life of her provinces during the last half century".[1] By 1862 (the writer adds) the romantic group known as the *Cuerda granadina* had already dispersed. Don Francisco, who must have heard of it as a boy, came into the world too late to share either in its abundant productive energies or its turbulent adventurous pleasures. The vigour of intellectual life in the provinces was declining rapidly; and yet, in this first volume of the *Revista Meridional*—there is a copy in the British Museum—may be seen how many flashes of genius there still were, and how great a part was taken by Giner in the common effort. The review must have taken up a good deal of Don Francisco's time during his last year at Granada. Next to Trinidad de Rojas, who performed the functions of editor's secretary, the responsible editor was Manuel Pineda, a painter "of rare talent but intense renunciation" and a man of somewhat "dionysiac" behaviour—qualities not infrequent in Granadino artists. Both were friends of Giner in his youth; and, in spite of being separated from them in after life, he always thought of them with real affection.

But for anyone who knew the Master personally, it is obvious that, if the *Revista* was put together among friends—those already mentioned and others whose signatures appear in its pages, and who were also his friends—and it had to be like that, for Don Francisco never undertook a piece of work in common unless it *was* among friends—then he must have already begun (as may be seen from opening the *Revista* anywhere) his favourite practice of intervening objectively in every moment and every detail of the common work, even to the very smallest detail, though he avoided appearing in public and kept himself in the background as much as possible.[2]

[1] *Obras completas*, III, x, introduction by M. B. Cossío.
[2] *Ibid.*

Cossío considers that Don Francisco's part in the *Revista* was not limited to what is usually understood as collaboration. He was not merely one of the contributors; the whole idea of the review shows that his part in it was decisive. The interest of this is not so much that the *Revista Meridional* was the first review to print anything written by Don Francisco, as that it was the first piece of corporate work which, without telling anyone or letting it generally be known, he really carried upon his own shoulders. This was always characteristic of him; he was never without some piece of work—or, better, several pieces of work—in which he was unobtrusively helping other contributors.

The *Revista Meridional* contains the earliest pronouncements of Giner on the philosophy of law, his special study, and a quantity of short notes on different subjects, principally notices of new books and of academic, scientific and literary events. All of these confirm the suspicion that it was Giner himself who watched over the make-up of the paper—his first literary and educative undertaking—and saw it safely through the press, and he did so with that "minute and inexhaustible assiduity" which he put into everything he undertook. Those who ever saw him (says Sr Cossío) ardently engaged in this way, can imagine his suggesting to Pineda that it would be a good thing to have some translations of foreign articles on electricity and magnetism; then writing to the orientalists Simonet and Lafuente Alcántara for articles on that peculiar variety of Spanish literature which was written in Spanish words but in Arabic characters; asking the great scholar Milá y Fontanals for an essay on Cervantes or a translation of Horace, and the poet Ruiz Aguilera for one of his elegies or some proverbs. Then there were obituary notices to be written; notes on new academicians; Campoamor, the satiric poet, or Valera the novelist; forbidding articles on questions concerned with algebra, full of pages of equations; spaces to be filled in by himself when the copy was short and there was not enough for the requisite number of pages. Then there came "the arrangement of all this luggage on the two main platforms which were to be the points of departure not only of the *Revista* but also of the emotion which it caused in its readers". One direction was serious and full of substance: chapters on aesthetics written by Fernández y González, aesthetics not for recreation but regarded strictly from a metaphysical standpoint. On the other side of those metaphysical pages were little poems: "Blanca", "The Cross by the Lake", "The Flower of Innocence", "The Two Lights", "The Star of the Sightless", "The Pearl of Algeciras Bay", "Antón and Juanita". Those who idolize romantic Spanish literature may read these poems in the British Museum; for others, the names are enough.

Such was the mental background of the generation of 1868; and the *Revista Meridional*, which ceased publication as soon as Don Francisco left it, is a precious document for giving us an insight into the origins of his personality. "In it there appear, clearly defined already, the main lines of his intellectual labour: the philosophical spirit, the passion for education, the varied interests and the inextinguishable curiosity for all sorts of things; a curiosity which he maintained until the end of his life, and which, being renewed every day, brought him the gift of eternal youth, because he always lived in the present."

Don Francisco, when he appeared in Madrid in 1863, appeared as a young man who cultivated literature and the law, both of them from a distinctly philosophical standpoint. He examined the foundations of authority as a question of political science, and discussed the characteristics of contemporary literature by applying principles, analysing concepts, laying works on the dissecting table, following the evolution of ideas and not merely recounting facts. He always said that he had no interest in history, if by history was meant the mere narration of events; yet he had actually been appointed to Madrid in the first instance to prepare a calendar of the historical documents in a government office, and for some time he had the correspondence of Philip II in his hands in the archives of the *Ministerio de Estado*, or Home Office.

One of Giner's earlier literary efforts was a review of *La Fontana de Oro* (*The Fountain of Gold*), the first novel of Pérez

Galdós. The review is unimportant in itself, but what mysterious voice can have whispered to Don Francisco the name of Pérez Galdós as a winner? It looks as if he had had it straight from the Parnassian racing stable. In the whole course of his life he only wrote four pages on fiction; but his choice fell precisely upon the writer who just then was preparing to produce, and to produce triumphantly, that immense series of novels which are among the most profound and permanent of modern Spain.

He was a member of the Athenaeum, *el Ateneo de Madrid*, a society which performs for Spain something of the function of the Union Societies at Oxford and Cambridge and other universities—a debating society and a club, a "Holland of free speech", an institution to which foreign correspondents in Spain have never ceased to give too much importance because they have always misunderstood its intentions. Giner seems never to have taken part in an Athenaeum debate; but as a speaker in the Philosophical Circle he soon won admiration and respect. His friend Colonel Luis Vidart—an officer in the artillery, an enthusiastic student of philosophy and writer on historical subjects—used to say to him affectionately when they were both old men: "My dear Giner, you are a criminal! You never ought to have done anything in this world except literature and public speaking". Even Salmerón, the political leader of the republic and for some time head of the government, re-proached him for not having dedicated all his powers to the greater good of his country—that is to say, to politics.

Yet the star which pointed the way to Giner was not politics, in spite of the influence of his uncle, Ríos Rosas. Nor was it literature. The influence which led him on was the teaching of Julián Sanz del Río.

There Don Francisco found, not a system of philosophy, but philosophy itself; and at the same time the object of his existence. For all philosophy must be lived, and lived with singleness of purpose, the supreme aspiration of a philosopher; it is not the painful struggle to attune action to thought, but the attainment of the con-viction that, from the idea made flesh, action will flow in gentle and obedient streams. Sanz del Río was the master, Sanz del Río was the philosopher. Giner learnt to cultivate his own garden in teaching and in philosophy. The devotion in which he held Don Julián was ineffable.

Full of enthusiasm for Sanz del Río, Don Francisco stood for a professorship at the University of Madrid, the *Universidad Central*, founded on the closing of the historic university of Alcalá de Henares in 1833. The professorship was that of the Philosophy of Law, and was to be awarded as a result of competitive examination. Don Francisco was the successful candidate but he had to wait for a year; the nomination was held up by the Ministry. In 1868 he was elected. But the moment he had been admitted, he wrote saying that his sympathies were with Sanz del Río, Salmerón and Fernando de Castro, who had been removed from their posts ("separated from their chairs") by the reactionary minister, Manuel Orovio, whose zeal had just been rewarded with the title of Marquis. By the end of the year, the fountain of honour, Queen Isabella II, had herself been separated from her chair; and the Marqués de Orovio had retired into private life, ready to appear and dismiss university professors again, as soon as the monarchy was restored in 1874.

The government formed by the triumphant revolution of 1868 restored all the persecuted teachers to their positions, and a decree was published that henceforth all primary education should be free. In the period which followed—"lively and enthusiastic" it was described by someone who went through it as a boy—the period which lasted from the departure of Isabella II in 1868 until the arrival of Alfonso XII in 1875, Don Francisco Giner took no public or conspicuous part, and he did not even join any political party. Yet he was known to most of the men who came prominently before the public, and was the friend and counsellor of many of them. He was really the soul of all the reforms which were carried out then or afterwards. And although his philosophical and social ideas naturally placed him on the side of those who had definitely broken with the monarchy, "radical as none other, but anti-revolutionary on principle", he had no sympathy for the extremist solutions which were then under consideration. The only occasion on which he appeared on the political platform was as a supporter of the candidature of Salmerón.

The moral influence of Don Francisco in the convulsions which shook the country at that time may be judged from the fact that he and one of his friends (Maranges) drafted the first paragraph of the Liberal Constitution of 1869—a declaration of individual rights. Again, in 1873 when the Minister of Justice was Salmerón, Don Francisco worked unceasingly for prison reform in collaboration with the greatest Spanish woman of the nineteenth century—Concepción Arenal. Even after the restoration the influence of Giner was noticeable. An undersecretary at the Ministry of Justice was a friend of his, and they often discussed constitutional questions. A remark dropped by Don Francisco at one of these conversations was passed on to the Prime Minister, and the reform it suggested was introduced into the legislation governing the composition of the Upper House.

However, with the return of the Bourbons, Don Francisco, like many others, suffered a profound disillusion.

After some seven years in which (as *The Times* neatly expressed it) revolution and liberal reform had been too closely identified to be stable, a bitter reaction brought into power the conservative clerical government of Cánovas del Castillo. The Carlist war was ended; unrest was put down. But the price had to be paid; and the price was fifty years of oppression and clerical control of education.

Liberalism! It is difficult to realize the terror once inspired by that word, or the means taken to root it out from among the faithful.

As the Virgin Mother of the Saviour of men crushed with her pure feet the head of the infernal Serpent, so Pius IX will also crush with his Syllabus the head of Liberalism, the true Serpent of the nineteenth century.

This blasphemous piece of rhetoric appeared in a Madrid newspaper of 1871;[1] while an "Appendix of Modern Errors"

---

[1] *Annual Register*, 1871.

was added to the Catechism. The following questions and answers are taken from the most recent edition of this Catechism, still in use in the Church of Spain: *Nuevo Ripalda enriquecido con varios apéndices* (14th edition, 1927). The Seven Deadly Sins had grown into the "Eleven Deadly -isms". Darwinism at that time took a prominent place, and was followed amongst others by Atheism, Protestantism, Socialism, Liberalism and Freemasonry. Darwinism was condemned because it was "a system both ridiculous and absurd". What did it teach? That men were descended from monkeys, of course (an answer which would have been given "o" in any examination paper in northern Europe). Hardly more fortunate were the answers on Atheism; their refined cynicism might escape the innocence of the pupil, but could hardly be hidden from the bitter experience of the teacher. "How do you prove the existence of God?" "The admirable working of the universe demonstrates it, and the agreement of all peoples confirms it." "What does Liberalism teach?" "That the State is independent of the Church." Three grades of liberalism—of independence—could be distinguished; but the Church had condemned them all, in the encyclical *Quanta cura* and in the *Syllabus*; the State should be subject to the Church, as the body to the soul, the temporal to the eternal. Was it certain that the Church should not meddle with politics? Most certain; provided that politics were contained within their just limits, and did not meddle with religion. Among the other false liberties of liberalism was the liberty of conscience. Was it true that a man could choose any religion he liked? No, for he ought only to profess that which was catholic, apostolic, Roman—the only true religion. What was the meaning of liberty of worship? That government should support the free exercise of all forms of it, even if they were false. The obligation of government, however, was to support true religion, which was the Catholic faith. But should it not support and protect all the opinions of its subjects? Yes, *señor*, always provided that those opinions were not condemned by the Church. (Horrid proviso!) The liberty of the press was condemned even more outspokenly. Ought the government to repress this liberty by means of the censorship? Evidently. Were there any other pernicious liberties? Yes, *señor*; the liberty of education, liberty of propaganda and liberty of meeting. Why were these liberties pernicious? Because they served to teach error, propagate vice and machinations against the Church. Did the Church tolerate these liberties? No, *señor*: for on repeated occasions it had condemned them. Was the Church then opposed to progress? The Church was opposed to the progress of error; but it had always fomented both the progress of truth, and true progress. Did the Church place obstacles in the way of liberty? The Church placed obstacles in the way of liberty of vice, but fomented the liberty of what was good and virtuous.

But there was more to be learnt about liberalism when the catechumen had answered all these questions; he had to be instructed on liberalism morally considered. What kind of sin was liberalism? It was a most grievous sin against faith. Why? Because it was a collection of heresies and errors condemned by the Church. Was it licit for a Catholic to call himself a liberal? No, *señor* (but, by a curious misprint, this answer ended in a question mark). Why? From the scandal caused by taking the name of an error condemned by the Church. Then as to newspapers: Did he sin grievously who subscribed to liberal newspapers? Yes, *señor*. Why? Because he contributed to evil with his money, put his faith in danger, and set a bad example to the rest. Was it at any time only a light sin to read the liberal press? Yes, *señor*, if occasionally one read news items or articles which were only slightly dangerous. Yet it was wisely pointed out in a note that if it was necessary to read part of a paper, for instance the Stock Exchange news, there was no reason on that account to read all the rest. Seven rules were then given for recognizing liberal papers; but the seventh rule was the most certain: to see whether, in relating events connected with the Church and its enemies, they remained "neutral". What ought one to do, then, in relation to the press? Extirpate the impious and liberal, while subscribing to and propagating the catholic. Lastly, as to parliamentary elections, the question was asked:

What sin is committed by him who votes for a liberal candidate?

And the answer was:

Generally a mortal sin.[1]

How strange and curious is this little book, *The Tablet* remarks. "In a few pages it answers all problems, furnishes all explanations, resolves all doubts and prepares for all the eventualities of life." Such, indeed, was the atmosphere in which Spanish educationists found themselves. This was what the youth of the Spanish nation was brought up to believe and to do, from 1876 to 1931.

One of the government's first cares after the restoration of Alfonso XII was to pass a series of Test Acts, and to force them unflinchingly upon the high schools and universities. In consequence, a considerable number of teachers who refused to submit, including some of the most eminent names in Spain, were ejected from their chairs and imprisoned.

One of the most noteworthy victims of this reactionary vigour was Giner de los Ríos, a man who had steadily kept aloof from any active part in politics, but of great weight among the more serious and disinterested of the republican reformers.

This is the account given by *The Times* (2nd October, 1884), in one of the numerous articles which, in those days, it devoted to the progress of Spanish education. It will be instructive to turn to the files of *The Times* at the moment of Don Francisco's arrest in 1875; for its correspondent was, needless to say, well informed, and not likely to be intimidated by the "traditional obstacles".

THE SPANISH GOVERNMENT AND THE PROFESSORS

Madrid, Ap. 3 (1875)

On the night before last, at half past 2 after midnight, Señor Giner de los Ríos, Professor of Filosofía del Derecho, or Natural Law, in the University of Madrid...received a visit from the police. He was ordered to rise from his bed, dress and make ready to leave Madrid by

[1] *Nuevo Ripalda enriquecido con varios apéndices* (14th ed. 1927), 117.

the 5 o'clock morning train to Cadiz, whence, it was understood, he was to be transported to the Canary Islands.... He was thus marched off to the Gobernación, or Home Office, in the Puerta del Sol, where, after being duly entered into the books of the police, he was (with two other political offenders bound to the Island of Fernando Poo) conveyed to the Atocha Station and accommodated with a seat in the Southern train on his way to his destination beyond the seas.

Sr Giner is a quiet, modest, retiring man, a good Catholic, who never meddled with politics, and was little heard of beyond the limits of his academical sphere. But he was set down, with Castelar, Salmerón, and others, among those theorists, optimists, or utopists whose teachings were represented as having sown the seeds of religious and political Liberalism in the schools, and countenanced a reckless and somewhat riotous spirit among the students—one of those "*Idéologues*", who, according to the first Napoleon, are "the pests of the State, at the bottom of all revolutions". Between these mere dreamers and the Government of Queen Isabella in its darkest reactionary period there had been incessant conflict; the University of Madrid, as in all other cities of Spain, France and Italy, was looked upon as the vanguard of the Revolutionary Army, and when Isabella fell, she was supposed to have succumbed to the enmity of the Professors, some of whom, in fact, were found at the head of the movement and wielded the destinies of the country through its various phases of anarchy from September, 1868, to December, 1874.

The article goes on to describe the decree of the Finance Minister, Orovio (26th February, 1875). All teachers in the institutions dependent on the State were bound to the strict use of approved text-books; professors were called upon to submit a synopsis of their lectures to the Rector of the University, who was to see that they contained nothing at variance with Catholic dogma, sound morals or monarchic principles, nothing, in fact, which would tend to the development of "fatal social errors". This circular,[1] *The Times* observes, was a mere repetition of the Decree of the 24th October, 1824, by which Calomarde, the minister of Ferdinand VII, ushered in an era of intellectual darkness after the defeat of the constitutional party. A French

---

[1] It will be found in García Carraffa, *Azcárate*, 77 ff.

army, known to fame (or at least to fiction) as "The Hundred Thousand Sons of St Louis", and commanded by the Duke of Angoulême, had marched into Spain unopposed, barely ten years after the Duke of Wellington had so laboriously pushed the French from Portugal to the Pyrenees. Liberals were everywhere arrested, and one hundred thousand crusaders were apparently needed for the defence of throne and altar, the principle of absolutism, and the prevention of "fatal social errors".

"In other countries", *The Times* remarked, "it is found that teachers had best be implicitly trusted, as liberty seldom fails to correct its own abuses." But, in Spain, things were different. Castelar threw up his lectureship at once. With Castelar went Salmerón; and many others would have followed, had not their private circumstances prevented it. These, without actually resigning their chairs, sent in more or less outspoken protests to the Rector, "and it was to a letter in the same sense that Sr Giner was indebted for the visit of the police to his bedside the other morning and his hurried voyage to the Fortunate Isles...".

The correspondent of *The Times* did not think it well to go into greater detail; but it is stated on unimpeachable authority that when Cánovas del Castillo, the Premier, became aware that a protest had also been received from Francisco Giner, he sent an under-secretary to him with the following message:

Diga a Giner, por Dios, no haga caso. Todas esas cosas del decreto de Orovio no tienen valor. No se hará nada.

(Tell Giner, by God, to pay no attention. All those things in Orovio's decree are worthless. Nothing will be done at all.)

Don Francisco's reply was:

Dígale V. que se lo digan en la Gaceta.

(Tell him that they should say so in the *Gazette*.)

This touched Cánovas on a tender spot; it was his wounded pride which sent the police to Don Francisco.[1]

"Those disputes between the Government and the University,

---

[1] Information from a contemporary.

between the priests and the professors," *The Times* correspondent observes, "contribute in no small degree to perpetuate political agitation in Spain...and other Latin or Catholic countries, one party declaring that Science is undermining the whole basis of public morality, the other contending that religion is stopping the way of all scientific advancement."[1]

Don Francisco was imprisoned in the Castle of Santa Catalina at Cadiz, a forbidding fortress on the edge of the Atlantic. The British consul, Thomas Fellowes Reade, went to see him, and is said to have offered him his support and that of public opinion in England. This, however, Giner refused. "A Spanish Government", he said, "has put me in prison; and a Spanish Government must get me out." He made friends with a Scottish family, one member of which, Joseph Macpherson, was a geologist who afterwards lived in Madrid, installed a geological laboratory in his own house and took classes for Don Francisco. He was the author of several geological works published in Spanish, and amused Don Francisco by declaring that he had never had to sit for a single examination, or obtained any academic distinction in his life.[2] His name has been cut, as a memorial, on one of the pillars of the "Geologists' Well" in the Sierra de Guadarrama.

Another friend of that time, Arcímis, was also interested in science. He was an astronomer, a Spanish Sir Robert Ball, whose book *El telescopio moderno* did for a whole generation of Spanish children what *Starland* did for us in England. In after years in Madrid, he set up a little observatory for Don Francisco, on the roof of his house. Proposals were made for founding a free Spanish university in Gibraltar (which would have been of the greatest benefit to Gibraltar, at any rate, if not to the rest of Spain); but eventually Giner was allowed to return to Madrid, and there, with the help of other lecturers who had also been "separated from their chairs", he was able to put into practice a scheme which had been in his mind from the first moment of persecution.

[1] *The Times*, 10 April, 1875.
[2] F. Giner, *Ensayos de Educación*, 128 (note).

He gathered together a little band of kindred spirits and in 1876 founded the *Institución Libre de Enseñanza*, or Free Educational Institute, which thus took its rise as a protest against State and clerical control of education. According to its own statutes, it was a private association held entirely apart from the spirit and interests of any special religious communion, philosophical school, or party. It received no subsidy from the State or any public body; what funds it had were derived from shares subscribed at a very low rate of interest.

"As the principal founders of the Institution belonged to the higher branches of education, it naturally began as a private university college. It was soon found needful, however, to add preparatory classes, and, as the venture extended, its moving spirits became convinced of the necessity of applying all their available forces to improving elementary education, at the same time that they found themselves free to carry out their own scheme of reform. The original Institution was thus transformed into a complete day school which [eight years after its foundation] numbered rather over 200 boys, while the reforms of which it was the practical embodiment were so fundamental and so logically carried out as not only to make it a new departure in Spanish educational history, but also to give the experiment a European significance."

The Times correspondent described the curriculum in detail. He was particularly struck with the school excursions, which, he states, were carried out on a greater scale than in any other school in Europe at the time. In connection with the more important of these—to mining centres, for instance—special classes were held for a few days beforehand, so that the boys might be in a position to understand what they saw. "The excursion organization at the Institution has been brought to great perfection, and the boys in the higher classes have visited the chief places of interest throughout Spain; some of the walking tours in the summer even cross the Pyrenees. In this way boys of 12 at the Institution possess a knowledge, for example, of architectural styles that some architects might envy, gained by repeated visits to the most noteworthy buildings in Spain." The Institution abolished the irregular holidays on Saints' Days, and substituted a weekly half-holiday besides the Sunday. These, too, were often used for short expeditions around Madrid or for visiting factories.

This application of Froebel's "intuitive" method was carried much farther. The aim of the Institution was to give this form of teaching whenever possible, and whole courses of study, such as the history of painting and sculpture, etc., were followed exclusively in the Madrid galleries. The class met in the museum instead of in the school, and was conducted by the master in the actual presence of the pictures and statues. (There may seem nothing much in this nowadays, but it was new and revolutionary in 1876.) The same spirit reigned through all the teaching. The classes were small, so as to admit of lessons taking a free conversational form. Text-books were almost done away with, being substituted by the boys' own note-books. These were treated, however, very seriously, being regularly looked over by the masters. They formed the only work done at home, nothing being given out in the way of "prep.". Formal examinations were entirely abolished, the authorities at the Institution having the meanest opinion of their worth as a test of real education. Reforms in this independent spirit were carried into minute details. Thus, in the teaching of history, the ordinary process was reversed; instead of beginning with ancient history and working down towards modern times, at the Institution they started from contemporary history and worked backwards, which was found to ensure a more intelligent appreciation of historical continuity.

The Institution aimed at something higher than these reforms of educational procedure. Giner and his colleagues were profoundly convinced that the only hope for the regeneration of Spain lay in the spread of education in the broadest sense. But education, if it were to restore the vigour of mind and body lost by the devout inertia of two or three centuries, must do more than impart knowledge, even on the most improved principles; it must turn out men worthy the name. In thus boldly attacking the problem of all education at its foundations they were

brought to the conclusion that the form of education most
suitable for Spain must combine the completeness of the
German educational programme with the broad and humaniz-
ing spirit of the English. The Institution was at that time the
only school in Europe which openly sought to follow the spirit
and general lines of English education, and which aspired to
introduce open-air games, and the personal liberty which
accustomed a boy to "self-government". On the other hand,
in their resolute avoidance of cramming, they were content
that the quantity of work done should be smaller than in most
schools on the continent, though they contended that its
quality was higher. As regards moral training and supervision,
the Institution represented a complete revolt against the Jesuit
spying system or the French "subordinate staff of inspectors and
surveillants to relieve the masters of all but their teaching
duties". Those were entirely done away with, and the pupil's
progress was looked for solely from the personal intimacy in
which he lived with the masters during the day. Great attention
was paid to cleanliness and matters of personal care and refinement. There were no boarders at the Institution, but the influence of the masters succeeded in making a daily bath very
general among the pupils. Anyone who knew Spain fifty years
ago will understand that this means a great deal more than we
nowadays should be inclined to suppose. So free was the inter-
course between teachers and taught that it was common for the
masters to attend each other's courses in the ordinary classes with
the boys, and they joined freely in the games.

Looking back on the work of the Institution fifty years after
its foundation by Don Francisco Giner, it becomes clear that
the decree of Orovio, abolishing the freedom of university
teachers, has done more for the progress of Spanish education
than all the reforms proposed or carried through by the State.
Nothing would have changed without the work of this small,
independent group which carefully kept apart from the State;
and almost all the ideas of the Institution which at first caused
surprise and indignation, have been accepted by everyone, even
by the bitterest enemies of free education. It is a commonplace

nowadays that in education the essential thing is the personality of the teacher; that the child should be made to think for himself, and not (as was generally believed at that time) passively receive the ideas which were communicated to him; that the teacher should be, in his turn, someone who lives with his pupils; that games and physical exercises, handicrafts, drawing, music, excursions are an essential part in education; and that girls should be taught like boys, women like men. For some, the objection to the Institution has been the Krausist philosophy; yet, in spite of the objections which may be urged against Krausism from the standpoint of modern philosophic thought, it must be recognized that without that, the education of the Institution would probably have not proved so inspiring. "Education is a method; that which puts spirit into this method is philosophy. The philosophy of Krause gave the teachers at the Institution a lofty ideal and the power of persuasion which the teacher must possess in order to persuade in his turn. It has provided the firm foundation on which all spiritual labour must be built in order to endure.... Thousands of Spanish men and women, even some who have had no direct relation with the Institution, recognize that they are its debtors, not for a spiritual doctrine but for something which is more important still—for freedom of spirit."[1]

[1] *El Sol* (Madrid), 2 Nov. 1926.

V

DON FRANCISCO GINER (2)
The Wandering Scholars

DON FRANCISCO GINER considered that the chief problem of Spain was the problem of education. From first to last his mind was concentrated on the science and art of teaching, in all its aspects; and into that he put the full fervour of his devotion. Teaching was the great passion of his life; an intimate friend like Sr Cossío has no hesitation in saying that it amounted to something like a religion with him. Through devotion to his Institution, the *Institución Libre de Enseñanza*, he was able to carry on the work and apply the ideas of his master Sanz del Río: to make men and to bring knowledge within their reach, and his pupils and his companions followed him in the task. He felt for the Institution the passion of the creative artist for his work—for the work which he knows will be his masterpiece; and his mind was sufficiently supple to be always creative, down to the last moment.

The extent of Giner's influence can be seen in the progress of education in Spain, and more especially in the knowledge and understanding of the problems which have confronted the Spanish educator since 1882. In that year a National Congress on education met in Madrid, and the Institution emerged for the first and only time from its unobtrusive and silent labour. There was an obvious and melancholy contrast (a member of the Congress has recorded) between Giner, Costa and the "Institutionists" on the one side, and on the other the more backward representatives of the nation at large.

At the Congress, after Cossío and Costa had both spoken, in the midst of general hostility and misunderstanding, Don Francisco Giner made an extempore speech, the second and last public appearance of his life. It was a speech full of facts; full of nobility, sincerity and indignation. From that time onward there remained in his mind a melancholy distrust of any rapid influence on the multitude;

and it confirmed him definitely in the belief that the only honour-able—and possible—course of action lay in the slow and careful preparation, from their earliest childhood, of the men of the future.[1]

Giner left to others, chiefly to Azcárate, the task of reforming Spain by laws, by government action, by what is called in Spain "revolution from above"; that is to say "reforms of conservative tendency introduced by radical-rationalistic means, the opposite of English methods".[2] In the short revolutionary epoch from 1868 to 1875 an attempt had been made to in-troduce freedom, in education and religious worship, by loosening the grasp of the State monopoly and raising the level of popular culture; but at the restoration, the old fear of ideas returned in full force. "The Spanish eighteenth century, in comparison with the nineteenth, was more open-minded and less timid, wiser and more practical", Sr Castillejo remarks. The eighteenth century had never been afraid of ideas; it believed that the world was ruled by them. The nineteenth century, because it knew that the world was ruled by ideas, was terrified of them, especially when they came from England, France or Germany. Yet, in the nineteenth century, Spain still remained rationalist, still clung to the belief that the world was ruled by ideas after all; only it was no longer optimistic, as it had been in the eighteenth century. For now it saw in ideas not "lamps which could be lighted in the minds of men to free them from error and ignorance", but potential bearers of moral and spiritual contagion. As a result of this attitude, there came a tendency to sever connection with foreign countries; and a narrow religious and political nationalism took the place of the cosmopolitan outlook of the eighteenth century.

Don Francisco found this all very well, "very plausible and very convenient, and no doubt likely to give great results, given the quantity and even the quality of the means at the disposal of a government". But, considering the mental and moral condition of Spain at the time, he thought it better to influence the individual conscience of the Spanish people rather

[1] Cossío, *Boletín de la Institución Libre de Enseñanza* (1915), 37.
[2] José Castillejo, *Minerva-Zeitschrift*, Oct. 1928, 203.

than the constituted authorities, "to reform customs rather than laws, and to conquer social life rather than a political party".[1] The authorities, however, thought differently. On the fall of the first republic in 1875 and the restoration of the Bourbons to the throne, the professors were persecuted no less than the liberal press, and the frontiers were thrown open for the return of the religious orders. Reaction returned, as in the time of Isabella II, and republican thought turned to conspiracy and subversive agitation, which could only have been successful if the leaders had been unanimous. In the end there was neither unanimity nor revolution. Castelar declared that it was impossible to put things back as they had been in 1868 and 1873; history (he said) offered no example of a single generation of men making two revolutions. Pi y Margall had no belief in the possibility of union among the leaders; he demanded a previous agreement on the republican programme, establishing the autonomy of the different regions of Spain—autonomy even for municipalities—as a principle which had to be accepted before an understanding between the party leaders could take place. Salmerón had too vivid a recollection of the outbreak at Cartagena, and of the trouble caused by that little independent republic with its three men-of-war; he would not hear of a federal programme. Ruiz Zorrilla put all his hopes on a conspiracy in the army.

Meanwhile the religious orders set to work to gain control of the education of those who would one day form the governing classes. Many of the colleges which they opened led to the closing of others managed by private individuals, generally on broad-minded, liberal principles. As time went by the teaching staff came to be recruited almost entirely from those who had been educated in monastic institutions; and the military academies, the professions, the civil service, banking, the Cortes and the government came to be filled with men whose minds had been formed—or deformed—in an atmosphere of falsehood, bigotry and stuffiness which was without parallel in the rest of Europe, and which caused grave concern even to the

[1] J. Juncal, *Boletín* (1915), 70.

Vatican itself. Even the humane studies were made to stink in the nostrils of broad-minded men. The reason why so few educated Spaniards of to-day care to learn Greek (for instance) is that Greek studies became almost the exclusive property of the religious orders. Undergraduates at Salamanca, to whom Unamuno had to lecture as University Professor of Greek, in many cases barely knew the alphabet; while a boy of 17, taught at a good school in Spain, was still in the stage of a boy of 12 beginning Greek at a preparatory school in England. The design of the religious orders (so it seemed) was to gain possession of the State through the control of education. The monarchy was naturally their ally and their friend, if not actually in their service; and the governing classes and the army were rapidly being brought in. Outwardly the proceeding seemed to have no ulterior motive; the orders could point with pride to the number of secondary schools and other educational institutions founded and maintained by them; and in primary education (to which they attached less importance) it was easy to prevail upon the local authority to cease to pay its share towards the upkeep of the National School and give its support instead to a school kept by a religious order.

Meanwhile the universities were bound by regulations which choked all personal initiative. The "Napoleonic" conception of a university was adopted, according to which a university became an official bureau in the service of public administration and of the different professions. The first care was to establish a system of numerous and mainly *viva voce* examinations for the purpose of conferring academic degrees. These examinations were the same for all universities and all students; but they did not include so important a subject as modern languages.[1] Since the interest of the students was principally directed to the results of examinations, the method crept in of learning a text-book by heart. This led to the foundation of cramming establishments to push backward and idle men through their examinations. And it was not only the backward and idle. If a man could learn certain books by heart—in law, for instance—he was certain of

[1] Castillejo, *ibid.*

a career, which, if not remunerative, was enough to support him and a family as well. Under this system, no laboratories were built and no *Seminare* could be developed, as in Germany; the university appeared to young men "hateful as a prison". Professors and lecturers were inadequately paid, and a large number of them had to tire themselves out with other work before they ever came into the lecture room.

The results of this educational policy were clearly shown in 1909, in the ferocity of the attack on the enlightened but free-thinking schoolmaster, Francisco Ferrer, followed by his judicial murder on a trumped-up charge. Twenty years later there were groups of "Young Maurists", "Young Jaimists", "Social Defence", the "Sacred Heart", and the like—all of them forming parties of "action", and ready to use any kind of action, even violence, in order to support "their old schools". Under the restored monarchy the religious orders seemed to have won. In the press, in the family, in society, in politics, in business, in public affairs, in everything that represented influence, power and profit, the clerical "Right"(whose representative sat on the right in the Cortes and also considered that they alone, socially speaking, were the "right" people) were everywhere predominant, and their predominance was largely due to clerical control over secondary education. As to primary education, the interference of the Church, and the stultification by clerical intrigue of all government educational measures, led to a condition in which less than half (49 per cent.) of the population could read and write.

One thing, however, clerical education had not been able to achieve—formation of character. A convincing vote in favour of a republic had only to be given at municipal elections (as in 1931), and the "right", having "jerrymandered" the elections in country districts and bought votes in towns such as Cadiz (in which a strongly republican population unexpectedly voted royalist),[1] turned tail on finding themselves defeated and, in

[1] Miss Madge Macbeth, a Canadian lady who was in Cadiz at the time, states categorically that votes were bought by the "Right" for 15 pesetas apiece (*The Times Literary Supplement*, 25 Feb. 1932).

many cases, ran. The Archbishop of Toledo also ran, and was not allowed to return. The revolution of 1931 and the bewildered incompetence of monarchist and clerical forces—and to a certain extent, of republican forces as well—demonstrated finally and irrefutably the hopeless inadequacy of fifty years of education dominated by the religious orders.

One man alone—Giner—was able during these fifty years to free himself from political and religious bias, and seriously consider the fundamental problem of providing Spain with educated men capable of taking their places in the government. Thanks to him, to the Institution which he founded and to the spirit emanating from it, there is at last in Spain a generation of teachers who believe in free inquiry and tolerance, and even impose on reactionaries a certain respect for their opinions, because they possess the dignity of conscience of men emancipated from priestly tyranny.

No one better than Giner was able to adapt himself to the Spanish tradition. In religious and political questions he took up a position of strict neutrality, but not of indifference. He declared that every form of belief had the right to recognition, and protection. He would have banished from the schools every sign of division or hatred, and recommended that religious instruction should be given at home and in church, but not in school. He wished schools to be pervaded by a spirit which was religious but not sectarian, to form an atmosphere sensitive to philosophy and history which would awake the need for ideals and beliefs.[1] "He had an anti-revolutionary mind, a great veneration for any spontaneous embodiment of social knowledge, and a great love of nature, art and popular customs." He believed that an empire's greatness was not to be measured by the countries it had conquered but by the spiritual . values it produced; and so, for him, the highest point of Spanish life lay in the tenth and eleventh centuries, in which Spain was open to the spirit of tolerance and friendship for foreigners.

Giner believed that a true understanding of the backwardness of Spain was the first step towards improvement. After the

[1] Castillejo, *Minerva*, 206.

attempts at reform which had been made during the First Republic, he lost all belief in mere legislation; Spain could never be reformed by Act of Parliament. He trusted only to a slow change of heart, and consequently maintained that the fundamental problem of Spain was not a problem of the form of the State but one of national education. It was necessary to begin at the top. The first step towards a better education was the better training of teachers; and in order to promote this he proposed that permanent contact should be established with educational movements in other countries by sending young Spanish teachers and students abroad, while at home he envisaged the union of suitably trained men and women in small research circles so that they should be in a position to prepare the ground for others.[1]

As early as 1878, Don Francisco began to suggest to his assistant masters at the Institution that they should go abroad to see how their subjects were taught in other countries. In this way one of them brought from France the idea of the school excursions which became such an important part of the training at the Institution. Cossío, who desired a real humanist training, studied in Italy as well as France; when barely twenty, he went to the Spanish College at Bologna—the famous *Collegio di Spagna*, founded in 1365 by Cardinal Albornoz. He worked hard at the history of the fine arts, heard lectures by Carducci, the great classical Italian poet of the nineteenth century, and diligently observed the methods of teaching employed in the university. In 1880 he was present at the International Congress of Education at Brussels; in 1882 he spent some time in Germany. In that year an Englishman, who had been first a pupil and then an assistant master, introduced games into the Institution. He first persuaded the children, boys and girls alike, to play rounders; and then one day he appeared with a curious leather object which a boy called Antonio Vinent (now known by a distinguished name) helped him to inflate. It was the first football in Spain.

The Englishman was Stewart Henbest Capper (1859–1925),

[1] Castillejo, *ibid.* 206.

a man with a remarkable gift for friendship and for making people do things. He had been educated at Edinburgh and Heidelberg, and became in 1879 private tutor and then private secretary to the British minister at Lisbon, Sir Richard Morier. In 1881 Morier was transferred to Madrid, and Capper soon found his way to the Institution. He had had a good classical training and spoke several modern languages; but Don Francisco and Cossío saw with astonishment that he had no knowledge whatever of the history of art, and hardly knew one style of architecture from another. He went for excursions with the boys of the Institution, and heard Don Francisco talk about the Spanish cathedrals which they visited. Suddenly he began to draw, and showed such a passionate interest in the study of architecture, that after hard work with Don Francisco and Cossío he was able to become professor of architecture at Montreal and ultimately at Manchester; while the end of the European war (for which he volunteered, in spite of his fifty-five years) found him in the Ministry of the Interior at Cairo.

In 1884 Giner and Cossío paid their first visit to England. They had been fortunate in their few English friends; Capper had been a good representative of his country, and had a brother on the staff of *The Times*; the Innerarity family had been kind to Don Francisco in Spain, and his friend Azcárate had married one of the daughters. Further, there were the Riaños, both of them enthusiastic anglophiles and well known in London society. Juan Facundo Riaño, born at Granada in 1829, was an archaeologist and a historian of art, who was for a short time Director of Public Instruction. He did good work for training colleges, and especially the Museo Pedagógico Nacional, of which Cossío had been appointed director. In Spain it was said of him that he "contributed more than any other to rectify the education of Spanish archaeologists, by impressing upon them the value of personal investigation". In England he was known as the author of a valuable book on *Early Spanish Music* (published by Quaritch), and he had written the *Guide* to Spanish arts as represented in the collections at the Victoria and Albert Museum. Moreover, he had married a beautiful and cultured woman, Emilia de Gayangos, daughter of his former teacher of Arabic at the University of Granada. Doña Emilia had family connections in England; her mother had been English, and she herself was described as "the reigning beauty" of a London season, while her portrait painted by John Phillip was exhibited at the Royal Academy in 1856 and was engraved under the name of "Doña Pepita".[1] Another portrait hung in their house in Madrid—full of beautiful Spanish things and at the same time a Victorian "home"; it is now in the Museo de Arte Moderno. Doña Emilia's father, Pascual de Gayangos (1809–97), was an orientalist who held important posts in Spain; but he resided much in England, working daily in the British Museum, where he catalogued the collection of Spanish manuscripts. He was "very partial to this country": "Better than all the Murillos and Velázquez (he would say) is the English mutton leg", and the English friends who came to his house included Gladstone and Lord Ripon.

Giner and Cossío, therefore, had seen some of the results of English education, and were most anxious to make the acquaintance of English educational practice. It was founded (so they understood) "on the formation of character, and on games, regarded as an ethical force".[2] They could not foresee a time fifty years later, when games would have a hard battle to hold their own in school programmes, and when many parents do not believe that they strengthen moral virtues, observing drily that they cannot afford a son who only plays for his side.[3]

An opportunity was offered by the International Congress on Education held at South Kensington at the beginning of August, 1884. That year in England had not passed without excitement. Certain persons had acquired a habit of leaving handbags filled with dynamite in the cloakrooms of London railway stations, or at the bases of London statues and public monuments. The infernal machines did not always explode the dynamite, but the customs' officers bore down on anything in the shape of a handbag, while English ladies returning from Italy had to unpack

[1] *The Times*, 12 Oct. 1897.   [2] Cossío, *Boletín* (1915), 36.
[3] *The Times*, 3 Oct. 1932.

and display even their paintboxes, in case they contained dynamite or nitroglycerine.

The International Congress of Education was the beginning of Don Francisco's long connection with England. It was characteristic of him, that he agreed to Cossío and not himself being regarded as the official Spanish representative [1]; characteristic also of that representative, that he seldom spoke during any of the meetings, and did not follow the example of the Brazilian representative in giving a glowing account of educational progress in his own country. Cossío and Don Francisco sat quiet, keeping their ears and eyes open. The chair in one of the sections (Training of Teachers) was taken by the Hon. Lyulph Stanley (afterwards Lord Stanley of Alderley, and, from 1909 until his death in 1925, generally known as Lord Sheffield). Though he did not make the acquaintance of the two Spanish delegates on this occasion, he met them again in Paris, in 1889, at the celebrations of the centenary of the French Revolution; he became Don Francisco's strongest link with England, and visited Spain on several occasions himself. The ideal England, of which Don Francisco had always dreamed, seemed incarnate in this unobtrusive but indefatigable public servant; the ideal educationist rang in his speeches and writings: in his view of Denominational Training Colleges and Board Schools, his plan of Oxford University Reform, in his speech delivered at the meeting of the School Board for London on the proposal to alter the rule of the Board in reference to Bible teaching.

In 1886 Giner and Cossío "came under the inspiration" of Eton and Oxford. At the latter they had the good fortune to stay in Balliol as guests of the Master, Dr Jowett, to whom they had an introduction from Sir Richard Morier. Jowett was at that time Vice-Chancellor; and the Spanish visitors felt that they had been received "not only by the leading humanist, but by the most educative spirit of the time in England". They were present when honorary degrees were conferred upon John Bright, Robert Browning and James Russell Lowell, and afterwards made their acquaintance. Thus they completed,

[1] *The Times*, 4 Aug. 1884.

with a "direct vision" of English life, the influence which by means of the Riaños they had already received of "the refinement and poetry of English customs"[1]—the refinement and poetry, that is to say, of a Victorian English home. To the end of his life Don Francisco was in constant communication with friends in England, France, Germany, Belgium and Portugal; and he had devoted admirers in the United States.

In the political world of Restoration Spain the Institution had few friends. Many conservatives, though they showed no outward hostility, could not conceive how the idealism of Giner, with his deep moral and religious sense, his genius for friendship, his strict tolerance and his love of old-fashioned Spanish ways, could be so faithful an ally of those who were often branded as "godless" and "revolutionary". Their political leaders, however, refused to temporize with opinions which seemed to endanger religious unity and the predominance of the religious orders; and in Parliament, press and pulpit a campaign was opened against the Institution, which had hardly died down at the coming of the Second Republic. The Institution returned no answer; it even profited by persecution, for it was able to clarify some of its ideas and dispense with half-hearted supporters whose real interest was their own personal advantage. With the halo of persecution the ideas of the Institution spread through all ranks of Spanish society.[2]

The traditionalists of the Carlist and Catholic right wing rejected all the educational reforms of the nineteenth century, and the imitation of foreign models; nor did they recognize the right to teach science, which they believed to be the enemy of religion. The liberal and conservative parties, however, which regularly succeeded one another in office and represented an alliance between the monarchy, the Church and democracy, were willing to accept moderate reforms, but they distrusted freedom of speech and unlimited propaganda; moreover, they expected everything to be done for them—they had only to hold out their hands, and reforms would come straight from the statute book. The socialist parties demanded a drastic reform of

[1] Cossío, *Boletín* (1915), 36.　　　[2] Castillejo, *Minerva*, 207.

the primary schools, in order to cope with the problem of illiteracy: but they could not persuade the masses to take any interest in higher education, forgetting that teachers cannot be trained without an adequate provision of training centres; while the revolutionary groups which were in communication with foreign countries and foreign culture set their hopes on the destruction of the existing political system.

Support for the idea of "intellectual co-operation" between Spain and other countries—particularly Germany—was forthcoming from another quarter. Santiago Ramón y Cajal is a histologist who has won world renown for his work on the structure of nerve cells; yet his is a typical case of tenacious self-education in completely hostile surroundings. He learnt practically nothing at school or university. He was up in arms against the authoritarian spirit of Spanish education and knowledge derived entirely from books. He began his study of anatomy by secretly taking bones and limbs from the cemetery of his native village. At the end of his university career, his thirst for knowledge led him to read Lamarck, Spencer, Darwin, Wundt, Helmholtz, and even Berkeley and Hume, Fichte and Kant. Through his own efforts, he learnt modern languages. Although entirely without resources, he spent the small savings, from the lessons he gave, in buying a microscope, materials for microscopic research, scientific books and periodicals. On the top floor of his modest dwelling at Saragossa he fitted up a laboratory. In order to publish his first piece of research he learnt lithography, made his own reproductions of microscopical drawings and photographs, and even ventured to publish his work in editions limited to 100 copies. A professor at Göttingen was the first to recognize Cajal's merit, and he made the young man's work known through an international scientific journal. In 1889 the greatest histologists and biologists in Germany honoured Cajal for his discoveries; and he, on his side, beheld with astonishment the spectacle of the German universities with their academic freedom and their institutes for research. Cajal was a liberal in politics, an evolutionist in philosophy, an agnostic in religion, and the enemy of every form of dogma—religious, scientific or philosophic—that in any way hindered the development of an unprejudiced scientific conviction. Through the weight of his authority he had more right than any man living to point out how far Spain had dropped behind other countries in education, and to suggest means by which she might catch them up. In 1897 he appealed for direct research as an essential factor in scientific work, for which (as he said) the man, and not the means, was what really mattered. He recommended compulsory lay elementary schools; a selection of the most industrious pupils for higher education, and a reform in the universities, converting them from mere degree-conferring establishments, which only prepared men for the professions, into real centres of intellectual activity like the universities in Germany. Finally, being convinced that the backwardness of Spain was a consequence of its isolation, he proposed to send hundreds of Spanish students abroad, so that professors with their eyes glued to the past might gradually be replaced by younger and more inspiring teachers.[1]

In Spain (as sometimes also in England) things are still discussed when they are no longer being discussed in any other part of the continent. When Cajal appealed for funds to send students abroad, there were still many people in Spain who declared that there was no need for students to travel, and that much good might be learnt without ever setting foot outside one's native land. Don Francisco did not deny this, but he encouraged all studious young men to go abroad, only regretting that so few were able to afford the journey. "He would have liked a scholastic emigration *en masse*, like the Japanese at the end of the last century."[2] He was not afraid that Spanish students, by going abroad, would lose any of their national characteristics. On the contrary, he was afraid that they would associate too much with their own countrymen, and not share fully in the life of the country where they were. "He knew very well that on their return they would perceive the peculiar beauties of their own country with a comprehension and consciousness stronger than ever before."

[1] Castillejo, *Minerva*, 205.   [2] Pijoán, *Mi Don Francisco Giner*, 67.

The story of the Spanish wandering scholars of thirty and forty years ago, before the creation of travelling studentships, has been described by one of them. It was "worthy of the heroic times of Alcalá and Salamanca", when the students described in the *Exemplary Novels* of Cervantes had to walk half across Spain in order to reach their universities, and sometimes failed to get there altogether, drifting off to the wars in Flanders, the armies of occupation in Italy, the tunny fisheries of the Atlantic coast or a pretty face in an inn at Toledo.

They discussed with full knowledge the relative hardness of the seats in the third class carriages of the different countries in Europe, and they knew the nutritive value of every article of food, in proportion to its cost, better than all the graphs in biological laboratories.

It was a sacrifice; and besides, it was not so useful as it might have been. Not only was the student hindered by material preoccupations; his stay abroad was usually too short. He had to come back just when he was getting to know the professors, making friends among the students, becoming familar with the language and realizing what he ought to work at for preference. He came back sadly, without really having learnt much, and consoled himself with the fantastic illusion of going abroad again soon, to finish some piece of work which he had begun.

Still, when he returned to Spain he realized that he had not lost his time completely. How many things he had learnt without noticing them! He knew, at least, of the existence of certain problems, the relative importance of certain theories, the modern bibliography of his subject, and modern methods of investigation. If only he had the books at hand, and above all the complete sets of periodicals! He would almost have been able to go on with his work in Spain!

The company of Don Francisco consoled him in his dejection.... How anxiously he questioned the returned traveller! How impatient he was to obtain information!

"And tell me, what do they think now on such and such a point? What is the opinion on such and such a book? How far do they think over there that such and such a theory still applies?"

For days and days he would go on asking questions to get information for himself. As cattle-dealers when they value a sheep have only to pass their hand along its back, so Don Francisco would draw out with questions what the young student had learnt on his travels.[1]

At last, in 1907, a *Junta* was formed, with the primary object of sending students abroad with adequate means—the *Junta para Ampliación de Estudios*, or "Board for widening the scope of studies". It had a narrow escape; and came near to being suppressed when it had hardly begun.

"The liberal government which founded the *Junta* fell that same week, and was followed by the most wretched ministry of force which we have had since the disaster of 1898.... The new Minister would have put an end to the *Junta* if it had not been so ably defended by its secretary, Don José Castillejo, who succeeded in allaying the Minister's suspicions, and encouraging in him the belief that he, Castillejo, was a mere idiot, and the *Junta* an organization which had been born dead and only served to give doles to three or four poor pensioners, a thing of no great importance to a Minister of the Crown."[2]

Spanish learning can never be sufficiently thankful to Don José Castillejo; for the *Junta* would never have got through the difficult years of its youth, or the attack made on it under the dictatorship of Primo de Rivera by his grotesque Director of Secondary Education, who considered (for instance) that Oxford was all very well, but had nothing to show which could possibly be of any use to Spain, and that many of its essential features had already been tried and rejected in Spanish universities in the sixteenth century. When all friends of the *Junta* and sound education in Spain were in despair, waking every morning with the thought that they might read in the newspaper the decree of their dissolution, Castillejo, "with the calm natural to a man of La Mancha", knew how to keep silent, and wait for his opportunity.

The objects of the *Junta* will be best described approximately in his own words.[3] It consists of twenty-one life members. It is

---

[1] Pijoán, *Mi Don Francisco Giner*, 63–4.   [2] *Ibid.* 67.
[3] Castillejo, *Minerva*, 208–9.

an incorporated body—or "juristic person" (there speaks a man who has attended the lectures of Don Francisco Giner!)—with the rights of ownership and administration of property. It has a subsidy, and is a government department in so far as it applies public money to its ends. The first chairman was Ramón y Cajal; and various scientific and political divisions were represented on the Board. Among the original members were Menéndez y Pelayo, the well-known "polygraph", and his great pupil, Menéndez Pidal; Costa (see Chapter IX); Ribera, the orientalist; Simarro, the physician and psychologist; Sorolla, the painter; the jurists, Azcárate, Buylla and Santa María; engineering, chemistry, astronomy, medicine, economic entomology and education were also represented. "The *Junta* was therefore a kind of 'Peace of Westphalia' in Spanish culture." Men of opposite political and religious positions came together in it; priests and monks worked in its laboratories by the side of positivists and free-thinkers.

From the first, the *Junta* resolved to employ other methods than those of the nineteenth century. Above all, it sought to establish close relations with the science and the culture of other countries. In its first years, its activity was restricted almost entirely to sending students abroad. The selection was not made as the result of examinations. Each candidate had to state in writing his intentions, his previous education, his experience in teaching or in laboratory work, and his published or unpublished works. If any doubt arose, the *Junta* sent for the candidate and recommended him to undertake a piece of research in a laboratory, where he sometimes remained for several months or even years before he received a travelling studentship. In the first years of the *Junta's* existence, the government wished it to lay down what subject should be studied; this principle was soon given up; and complete freedom is now allowed for every student to study what he likes: a scientific, literary or artistic subject. The *Junta* selects those students who seem the best prepared, and gives preference to subjects which cannot be carried on for professional or financial objects. In order to obtain a studentship, a knowledge of the language of the country is demanded, in which the studentship applies. In 1910 a further step was taken. Count Romanones thought that the moment had come to introduce into Spain the modern forms of scientific institutions, and at the same time to make use of the men who had been trained abroad, together with researchers, who hitherto had worked in isolation and with restricted means.

The institutions which the *Junta* has founded no longer conform to the ideals of the nineteenth century. They confer no degrees or titles, neither do they hold examinations, nor provide any other advantage except that of quenching the thirst for knowledge.

They are something new in Spain, something without the dead weight of tradition which had always made it impossible to carry out any extensive reform in the Spanish universities. For this reason, the *Junta* and the "Centre for Historical Studies" provoked the hostility of some of the senior members of the Central University of Madrid. Their champion, the late Professor Bonilla y San Martín, was worthy of a better cause; the permanent value of his own work will live longer than his attack on the "Centre for Historical Studies", on the ground that it had "paralysed research within the university". The university had never encouraged research, nor had it ever been in a position to do so; the studentships in foreign universities alone provided the incentive and made possible the modern methods of work brought back by the returned students. Bonilla himself was a good scholar—in some ways a great scholar; but his development was due to his own efforts, and was in spite of the Spanish university system rather than because of it.

The *Junta*, the "Centre for Historical Studies", the pleasant residential colleges, the admirable secondary school, the "Instituto-Escuela", are all results of the work of Don Francisco Giner at the "Free Institution". Yet it would be a mistake to think that the Institution has itself grown into any of these things. It is (as its present director, Don Manuel Cossío, said) a kind of vaccine which has been injected into the official mind of Spain; or (as another authority expressed it) it has been "a ferment of renovation". It does not possess, nor has it ever possessed, a definite system of education which can be introduced by ministerial decree throughout the country. It is, on the contrary, a constant experiment, a direction, a tendency; a reform which is never finished; a perpetual example of the most daring educational principles in the face of the demand for practical utility, and, on the contrary, of the practical utility of every day in face of the highest principles. Some of the ideas defended by the directors of the Institution have been gradually extending through Spain, and may come in the end to be universally admitted. The ideas will triumph, but the Institution will not triumph with them. The social mission of the "Institutionists", like that of the Society of Friends, is always to be in a minority; but a minority which thinks of the future.

VI

DON FRANCISCO GINER (3)
The Lesson of the Master

"*¡El señor Profesor!*"

The voice of the bedell aroused us from our thoughts. We saw him come along the corridor: Don Francisco Giner. He was a little man; upright, with twinkling eyes, a clear forehead, and a stiff, white beard ending in a point, like the *hidalgos* in portraits by El Greco. He looked very neat and correct; but he was smiling. Attractive to the last degree. He came up to us, greeted us like persons for whom he had the highest consideration, stretched out his small, nervous hands in yellow gloves, and courteously invited us to follow him into the lecture room. Needless to say, we did so, with good will, enchanted by such a friendly welcome.

"My friends," he began, after seating himself amongst us, "I want to deserve well of you: and my greatest grief will be not to do my fair share in this work of culture which we are all here to undertake in common. I do not keep an attendance-list, or examine; so your presence at these lectures is absolutely voluntary. I regret that I cannot offer you my text-book, for I have none, and I leave it to the choice of each one of you. As to the syllabus, I have had it printed, and I beg you kindly to accept it."

We accepted copies, and could not fail to think of the difference between our new professor, and others who had converted this business of text-books into an easy way of making money. Then there began a dialogue, spontaneous and admirable; real teaching. We realised that we were in a new world. We came to have for Giner an affection and a devotion which ran to wild enthusiasm. Giner knew everything, foresaw everything; and he did so in such a way that, while he eased brains which had become stiff through having to learn so much by heart, he hewed and chiselled our intelligences with a redeeming and illuminating energy. The philosophy of law, which had seemed to us something abstract and unsympathetic, now appeared as the science of the good and austere life, and we understood the truth of that saying of the Master of

Masters, Plato, ''On earth, only the philosopher can be a good man''.

This is the recollection of a law student who attended Giner's lectures at the university about 1880.[1] The figure of Giner de los Ríos rises from the memories of university men with a halo of sympathy and respect. Spanish university life in those days was cold and unfriendly; it did not as a rule create lasting bonds of affection. "The university was like one boarding-house the more, through which passed generations of students who afterwards took flight and spread themselves over the offices and occupations of life, without carrying away from that land-lady (who after all was the official representative of Minerva) a recollection more cordial or more lasting than that of other landladies with whom chance had thrown them...."[2]

What struck everyone who attended Giner's lectures was his power as a teacher. "Good teachers were not always to be met with", Sr Diez Canedo observes; "they were seldom to be found in our lecture rooms. There were, of course, the eminent men who initiated you into the rudiments of a subject and the methods of studying it, who started you off and enabled you to go on working by yourself. There may have been teachers among them, but they were few; for a teacher is not anyone who would like to be, but someone who has come into the world with the gift of teaching. A teacher may be a man of no letters, and it is well known that great savants are not usually great teachers as well.... A good teacher is one who awakens something that sleeps; who widens the horizons of life and thought; who, perhaps without teaching anything definite, reveals to his pupils something of their own personality; who makes them realize the direction most in conformity with their own nature and decide to follow it without fainting."

Of such was Don Francisco Giner.

He was not a man like those we see every day. His appearance recalled the figure of St Peter in the "Burial of Count Orgaz" (by El

[1] Antonio Zozaya, *Boletín de la Institución Libre de Enseñanza* (1915), 64.
[2] E. Gómez de Baquero, *Boletín* (1915), 75.

Greco), reclining on clouds and with the keys of heaven dangling from his fleshless fingers.

A conversation with that man was something which filled you with terror—and consolation. He seemed to come out of himself, to pour the whole of himself into the mind of the person to whom he was speaking. Every question you asked opened up unlooked-for views in perspective; and you were often surprised because the answer you gave was generally something which it would never have occurred to you to say, being, indeed, one of your most intimate thoughts.[1]

These are the views of men who attended his lectures at the university. A stranger who arrived with a letter of introduction might have a somewhat casual reception.

He came up to me reading my letter of introduction; and hardly noticing me said:

"And who are you, and what do you want to do?"[2]

But the stranger would be pressed to stay to supper—a thoroughly Spanish supper (in which the garlic was not forgotten), but served in an English way, with flowers on the table. Whatever the apparent subject of conversation, the stranger could not but feel that he himself was the principal object of interest, and that Don Francisco was alternately interested and amused by what he said. All the time those "sparkling, scrutinizing eyes" would be fixed on the visitor. Those eyes, which were "dark and rather sad", surprised anyone who spoke to Don Francisco for the first time. No one could say that there was mockery in them, for a moment; but there was that kind of intense seriousness which made some people doubt whether the owner was quite so serious as he seemed. He looked right through you; and as you were painfully aware of the gaps in your knowledge or, in other words, of your appalling ignorance and your incapacity for anything like sustained and real thinking, you felt sure that he had divined your insufficiency, that his questions might be merely ironical and that he was only leading

---

[1] E. Diez Canedo, *Boletín* (1915), 60.

[2] J. Pijoán, *Mi Don Francisco Giner*, 8.

you on to give yourself away. That was not so, however. Don Francisco liked analysing young men; and by asking them questions, he obliged them to clear up points which they had left in doubt.

"Oh, no, no! It's too early for you to leave us." But the stranger would see Don Francisco's head falling forward, nodding. Was it one of those deep silences which used from time to time to interrupt Don Francisco's lively conversation, or was he merely going to sleep? And next morning it would be: "Come along, come along, I have to go to my lecture. Of course, you will not learn anything there—a person like you!— but you will see those boys, and they will be glad to see you".

At the lecture, he did not fail to present the stranger more or less in this manner:

You will forgive me, but this man dropped on me, from Galicia or Catalonia or wherever it is, just as I was going out. An unexpected pleasure, eh? And since then he has not stopped talking for a moment. The things I have had to listen to! Here is the man who has translated so-and-so, and written a book on something else, and knows more than anyone else about... whatever it is. And the proof of that is that they have made him secretary of the club in his native village—a position which he fills honestly enough, except that until the other day he didn't know how to wash himself, and I had to show him how to clean the ink off his fingers with salt of sorrel.[1]

The stranger could not help laughing, and he saw smiles on the faces of the class. Turning to his visitor, Don Francisco went on:

Do not be surprised if I have mentioned this about washing. Here we are studying the notions of Plato on Natural Law. For three months we have been reading him; and as there can be no doubt that, if we study him hard enough, Plato will be here in the midst of us, we must come to these lectures as well-washed as we can possibly be, physically and mentally. How disgraceful, if Plato were to come

---

[1] *Sal de acederas*, a method invented by Don Francisco, and one which has not been used since his death.

in now, and find one of you with dirty books or with the vicious habit of biting his nails!...

Come now; Sr Quiroga, will you go on with the discourse you began yesterday on the difference between phenomena and noumena, things in themselves?[1]

The boy would begin with a certain hesitation, in spite of the notes which he held in his hand; a skilful interruption by Don Francisco would help him out and put him at ease.

Far more intimate are the memories of those who were his pupils or companions, his boys or his masters, at the Free Institution. According to their different points of view, he seemed to some a Socrates, to others a St Francis. The austerity in him was tempered by charm of manner; his most abstract thoughts seemed works of art. "There were certain fine edges of delicate intimacy about him", one of his pupils has remarked; "an Andalucian polish. He was universal, and at the same time a man from Ronda; firm but yielding, master and companion, a model of sanctity and the friend of sinners; wise, just and good, and above all, human."

These phrases occur in the recollections of Don Luis de Zulueta,[2] afterwards Minister for Foreign Affairs in the republican cabinet of Don Manuel Azaña. It may be interesting to pursue them farther, for they give an intimate picture of Don Francisco in his daily round at the Institution.

Don Francisco taught more out of school than in. A class was a conversation conscientiously prepared; but every conversation was an improvised class. He never missed a class, if he could help it. If by any chance he did so, or if his lectures at the university were interrupted, he would collect his pupils on another day, in another place (as lecturers and undergraduates used to do when the universities were closed in the last days of the monarchy) and go on until the work was finished.

"It's entirely for my benefit", he would say. "I don't know whether you will have learnt anything by the end of term, but I am learning so much!"

[1] Pijoán, 15–16. [2] *Boletín* (1915), 45–56.

There could have been no greater example for his pupils than the way of life of this man, "who tried to learn something in every hour that he lived, to puzzle out some private contradiction, to increase in wisdom, always perfecting himself with silent effort, with exquisite care and even with a certain holy coquetry (*con cierta santa coquetería*) in the inmost parts of his soul".

Every day he seemed to become a little younger. The writings of his later years have greater ease and vigour than those published about 1870. His development as a teacher followed much the same course; "he passed from systematic thought and eloquent discourse, to work in common, flexible, complex, difficult, in which the teacher's words aimed rather at suggesting problems than at solving them".

"There is no ready-made formula," he said on one occasion. "The teacher should try different words for every idea, until one of them (who knows which?) may possibly evoke in the mind of the pupil a thought more or less analogous to that which the teacher has in his own mind."

At masters' meetings at the Institution, the opinion of Don Francisco on problems of education was generally the most radical and audacious of all. "Every day more radical, and every day a cleaner shirt."

"It was something," Don Luis de Zulueta continues, "to hear that little old man, with his sudden, bird-like movements, standing by the stove, and exclaiming:

'Of course, you all think differently; but then, I'm the youngest person present'."

Don Francisco seemed always accessible, always sympathetic, at any time of the day.

"I don't know, Don Francisco, if I dare say what I want to?"

"¡*Por Dios!* of course you can! With me, everyone dares. I divide the world into two groups; my friends and my intimate friends. The first are all men; the second—you people here, a few dozen. With the first, I forgive everything; with the second, I agree to everything. So that now you see... say what you like."

Attracted by his wisdom, and still more by his warm heart, there passed through Don Francisco's room persons of the most different kinds, and the most different shades of opinion. With his inimitable tact he influenced them all. "He was more interested in persons than in things, but he knew enough about all sorts of things to make himself interesting to all sorts of people."

Don Francisco talked a great deal, with an extraordinary mental agility and an inexhaustible variety of tone and feeling. He had no sooner dropped an affectionate confidence than he would be scientifically discussing one of the most impersonal and objective themes conceivable. As he remarked half in fun, he administered prodigally the holy sacrament of the word. He worked out his ideas in conversation with his friends and pupils, in which respect he differed considerably from Sanz del Río, his master, who would sit for hours in a chair, with head bent and arms folded, thinking. Don Francisco put his whole soul into every sentence. In spite of that, he was so simple in his words and his actions, so open, so like everyone else, that there seemed nothing of the superman about him; he was completely human. "Complete, ample, harmonious, his spirit was at home with all ideas; even for those most contrary to his own, he preserved not only tolerance and respect but even a certain mental hospitality. Ideas entered his head as friends did his house, without being announced; and his soul was open wide to the light of each new day."

Giner never tried to substitute ideals of his own for the ideals sincerely professed by another. For him, every thought was sacred—provided that it was really a thought. (So we can all remember our own masters: "Oh, Sir! I thought...." "What you mean is, you did *not* think!") Don Francisco tried to develop and perfect in each one the ideal which he had chosen. It did not so much matter what the man was, but why he was so.

You keep your ideas, and I will keep mine; he can keep his. The ideas are all different; but one thing they have in common—they are ideas.[1]

[1] Zulueta, *Boletín* (1915), 50.

So on another occasion he remarked:

I spent the afternoon with that great personage, the Marquis of R.; and (would you believe it?) we agreed about everything,...or almost everything. A pity there's an "almost", eh? An "almost" like that, which made us strangers for the greater part of the time, when we might be working together in so many things. But it's possible that that "almost" may be Spain itself.[1]

The attractiveness of Don Francisco's conversation lay to a large extent in the parentheses, the reservations, the limitations of his own idea. Whenever he explained a point of view, he always gave the views of the opposite side, and made his hearers see that there was much that was valuable and useful, much that could be respected, if not followed, in the opinion of others. Those were still days when it was possible to be "a good catholic but not clerical"—*buon cattolico ma non clericale*, to use the Roman formula, to belong to the Soul rather than the body of the Catholic Church. But Don Francisco's enemies were active and insidious. One day a plumber was urgently required; but the man had been "got hold of", and, once in the house, he put down his tools and began to make a speech. "I must warn you", he began, "that I am Catholic, Apostolic, Roman...." "Excellent, excellent," said Don Francisco, "I am delighted to hear it. That shows you know your job." Something in the look of Don Francisco, in the sound of his voice, completely won over the plumber, and he forgot the speech that he had been told to deliver and did the job very well, with a puzzled admiration for "that old uncle" whom he had been taught to believe was Antichrist himself.

Don Francisco had, of course, a supreme gift of getting on with people, that gift which the Spaniards call *don de gentes*. Yet he also had "a tongue in his head". It might be said of him (as was said of a certain university professor in England) that he had "the kindest heart and the bitterest tongue" in the university; and the occasional bitterness of his tongue only emphasized the kindness of his heart. Yet he was never sarcastic. Very few examples of his irony have been recorded; those who

[1] Pijoán, 59.

knew him are chary of repeating them, or repeat them in confidence; and rather than break that confidence, we must leave the bitterest things to the reader's imagination. Yet this is the side of him which gave point to the other; he would never have accomplished so much as he did, or have made so many friends, if his associates had not been afraid of saying silly things or making fools of themselves when he was present. The fear of ridicule is a potent force, in Spain as in England. Another difficulty with irony—as with abuse—is that it is difficult to translate, without explanation and footnotes; and when we try to think it in English, it becomes no more or no less than what many of us can remember from our own schoolmasters.

It was characteristic of Don Francisco to be "sparing in praise and ample and insistent in censure". He knew that the mind is always conscious of its faculties, but often blind to its defects; and since these spoil a man's work, upon them the master must keep his eye, so as to lessen them if he cannot get rid of them altogether. For Giner (Professor Altamira has written) every pupil was a possible creator, in science, in art or in life, and therefore a seed which ought to be protected from all danger. So the more he thought of anyone and the greater the faith he had in his future, the sharper was his criticism of the defects by which that future seemed to be endangered. Sometimes his tongue cut like a lash; but it generally saved a victim, owing to the energetic reaction which it produced. On one occasion he said to a pupil of his—a man of good understanding, facile pen, varied reading and the personal qualities which make for social success:

You will be what you like, because you have qualities enough and to spare to occupy what people call social position. What you will never be is a scholar.[1]

"He ridiculed our defects (another of his pupils has written) with an incomparable grace"; and his ridicule was so certain, that he often made more effect with a comic phrase than with a serious admonition. The word which we have deliberately

[1] Altamira, *Giner de los Ríos educador*, 47.

translated "grace" (when it might be "wit") led to an amusing
slip in Spanish by a devoted Portuguese admirer, the wife of
one of the masters at the Institution, who declared that Don
Francisco was "very greasy" when she meant "very witty"—
that dapper little man, with his cold bath and his clean shirt
every day, and his scrupulously neat and spotless clothing! How
Don Francisco laughed; for he adored the Portuguese, and was
adored by them in turn, because he admired their country and
understood their character. He had visited Portugal on several
occasions; he and his brother Hermenegildo had once composed
a guide-book for Spanish travellers in Portugal which included
"a masterly monograph" on the architecture of Batalha. "There
has been no better description of the beauties of the artistic
region of Batalha and Alcobaça", writes Sr Bernardino Machado,
once President of the Portuguese republic, and a devoted friend
of the Institution. And Don Francisco, who had made so close a
study of the industrial arts of his own country, had a "truly
rapturous" admiration for certain kinds of Portuguese pottery
(Caldas da Rainha), fine examples of which adorned his work-
room.

With what affection and regret, with what *saudades*, do I remember our interminable cogitations by his little writing-table![1]
The Institution became a second home to me: I believe that by this
time I must be the doyen of the honorary professors. For years in
those delicious autumn days of Madrid, I was a faithful devotee of
his enchanted dwelling; there I met all the leading Spanish person-
alities in art, science, education and politics, all overflowing with
sympathy for the claims of Portuguese democracy.

The marriage of Alice Pestana, a Portuguese social worker
and a writer of considerable talent, to one of the masters at the
Institution, brought her whole-heartedly into this cordial
movement of Spanish and Portuguese friendship. She ex-

[1] Portuguese is too musical a language to be strictly translatable into any
other. *Saudades* need a page or more of explanation and comment, while
the translation "little writing-table" suggests very much less than the
musical word *escrivaninha*.

plained the sweeping educational reforms undertaken by the new republic in her own country; and the example of the Portuguese care for juvenile offenders led her to found an institution in Madrid on the same lines. Alice found a firm friend in Don Francisco, and she needed one. Her generous, impulsive nature was deeply wounded by the attacks made on her country by some of the less reputable Spanish newspapers: and she flew to Don Francisco for comfort, which was never denied. Dear Alice! She had many friends; and it is something to have lived in the world and left with friends a memory of odd, unexpected sayings and quaint, naïve remarks, so that now they never hear or mention her name without an affectionate smile coming to their lips.

Yet Alice Pestana, in her quick, intuitive way, got very near the root of the matter, when she wrote on Don Francisco at the time of his death:

What was the secret of his teaching? Did he reveal anything new? Or was it that everything was transformed at the touch of his powerful creative imagination?

The secret lay as much in the form as in the substance.

As a philosopher, he set out on a road that seemed purely intellectual and abstract. But he carried us off to the flowery meadows of a philosophy which was completely human, a reflexion of real conditions of existence, with theories closely connected with the maxims which regulate life itself.

As a teacher, he brought us something that was the complete opposite of the old methods; and he discouraged the craze for oratory which has been so damaging to education in Spain. In his lectures at the University or at the Institution, he only aimed at one thing: to shake the pupil out of his torpor, stir him up to independent investigation, to working the thing out by himself; and above all he recommended games, art, the country.

As an educationist he created a complete system of social education, which had for its axis the child, the citizen, the *man* as he would like to see him, healthy in mind and body, and working for a Spain that was strong and dignified and which must one day rise again.[1]

[1] *Boletín* (1915), 82.

Don Francisco bridled his tongue in the presence of sensitive natures; but he could be severe with women when he liked.

In Spain, a woman meets with flattery more often than honest criticism. "But", Alice continues, "I had never met a friend like this!"

Sometimes there was a discussion. All of us dared now and again to disagree with Don Francisco, however strange that may seem to those outside the circle. And he, almost invariably, ended by saying to me severely, vehemently, in desperation:
"You're a sentimentalist!"

Again, there is the evidence of the Condesa de Pardo Bazán:

His advice, not without a certain sane severity, induced me to read and travel, to learn languages and read foreign writers; and at the same time to feel the poetry of the atmosphere of my own country, even of the things which were most homely and familiar.[1]

Don Francisco also had the power—for it is a power—of losing his temper, of reaching a pitch of exasperation which led him to fly out at those with whom he lost patience, and even to hit out at friends who tried to calm him afterwards. That did not happen often, and it became increasingly rare as he grew older; but it left him cast down for days. His resentment was often directed not so much against persons as against institutions, or persons in a public capacity representing institutions of which Don Francisco did not approve. "Thieves and prevaricators" in public places particularly exasperated him. He too (it was said) would have driven the money-changers out of the Temple, and he sometimes cursed the barren fig-tree with all the fury of an Andaluz gipsy.

I saw P. to-day (he exclaimed one evening). *¡Qué harapo de hombre!* What a filthy man! He came and asked me to go and beg M. for something or other. That thief thinks that everyone is in the same condition as he is!

[1] *Boletín* (1915), 57.

The words sound more abusive in Spanish than they do in English, as also do the following:

"What you have done is infamous!" he exclaimed to a boy whom he had caught in some act of dishonesty. "Unworthy of anyone who calls himself a man! Even your want of imagination offends me. There's not even hope of your being original."

"In his words he managed to maintain a certain circumspection and decorum; but his eyes scorched and blasted, like lightning, and the tone of his voice became almost insulting with hatred."[1] Yet it was hatred of the act, not of the boy; he abused things, not people, and always began by saying "What you have done", not "You are...". The result was that the culprit never felt the rebuke as personal abuse, "or if he did, it was like the rebuke of his own conscience". One morning on the platform of a tram, Don Francisco saw a man who had deceived him or been guilty of some characteristic piece of sharp practice.

"Don't you recognize me, Don Francisco? You don't say 'Good morning'?"

"It was because I did recognize you that I didn't say 'Good morning'."

Such outbursts were rare. Don Francisco generally achieved his ends by a gentle irony, which made people sharpen their wits when they were in his presence. The irony was given an extra twist in cases of pomposity. A Catalan had expressed his irritation at "the lack of moral greatness" in some of his fellow-citizens in Barcelona.

"Really now", Don Francisco exclaimed. "You are going to spoil us entirely! The day you are not pro-Catalan, you will lose the whole of your charm."

As a matter of fact, Don Francisco had a soft spot for Catalans as he had for the Portuguese. He understood them, admired their sterling qualities and could sympathize with their point of view; and for that reason there were many in Barcelona

[1] Pijoán, 44.

who adored him. The misunderstandings which from time to time have arisen between Catalans and Castilians (and which are apt to be exaggerated by foreign writers) have nearly always been due to absence of tact. A Catalan pupil of Don Francisco has some shrewd remarks to make on the question of tact in Spanish people. Tact was one of the faculties which Don Francisco most valued; he defined it as art in action, that is to say, aesthetics applied to conduct. It did not mean reserve or dissimulation, hypocrisy or deceit. On the contrary (this is a Catalan speaking, not Don Francisco), the best results were sometimes produced by frank direct statement. "Tact is a faculty which, for those of us who do not possess it from birth, is hard to acquire. I doubt whether in Don Francisco it was natural to his character." Don Francisco, however, certainly possessed the gift of tact, natural or acquired; while it is certain that some men for whom he had a great regard, like Costa and Unamuno, had never possessed the faculty of tact, and their efforts suffered from the lack of it.

"What a pity it is!" Don Francisco said one day. "There's Costa now. He was here yesterday. What a tragedy of a man! How many years—centuries perhaps—will it take for Spain to produce another man like that! And all that treasure of a great mind wasted through its own excess! But who has the right to say to a man like Costa: 'You ought to do this, or that; you ought to say more, or less'? Who knows if his roars of desperation are not what we most need in Spain to-day?"[1]

"May I speak to you for a moment," one of the innumerable visitors would ask, "or are you too busy?"
"Yes, very; busy talking."
As a matter of fact, talking was his best and greatest work. His custom (Sr de Zulueta tells us) was to read and write early in the morning. Then he had his bath, and did his room himself; breakfasted, and was ready for his day's work. "For", he used to say, "I begin to realize that my day's work is talking." In this way he had an influence on many persons with

[1] Pijoán, 45.

whom no one would have thought he had anything to do. Spain owes him "the best of the best things which have come since his time, in science, art, education or politics. No one ever gave such an impulse to the moral reform of Spain".

Don Francisco was not a man who looked back. Though he had lived through an entire period of Spanish history—romantic years as a student at Granada, his uncle Ríos Rosas, Sanz del Río, Salmerón, Azcárate, the Restoration, Orovio, the *Institución Libre de Enseñanza*, it was seldom that he could be heard to recall these episodes with the complacency of the old. He lived with his face to the future. He put his whole soul into every moment. For his pupils he constantly joined small things to great.

He gave us our conception of the universe and of the way to peel an orange.

There is scarcely anyone who was intimate with Don Francisco who does not remember, besides his teaching, some fond little detail, something he said or did. One day it was the pungent comment, answering in the same tone of voice but conveying an admonition which would not be forgotten; another day it would be the postcard with a single line of greeting, "affectionate as a hand-clasp at the right moment". Or it would be the memory of a day in the country, when he was over seventy: he climbed into a tree reciting verses and saying incoherent and enchanting things, "like a little bird with a spark of the pure spirit in its restless beak". There are people who have some small memory of Don Francisco, so insignificant that nothing in the world would make them say what it is; yet, to them, it is so great that they would not exchange it for all the Master's philosophy of law.

One of the things which Don Francisco enjoyed most was exploring Spain on foot, with chosen friends and disciples. He had regularly devoted his Sundays to the country, ever since he met the Riaños, from whom the suggestion must have come; and with them in 1876 he began to visit places near Madrid, especially El Pardo—the former royal residence, with its neat little Castilian town and pleasant palace, and the sunlit solitudes of the vast domain where Velázquez used to sketch the landscapes for his equestrian portraits of princes. He also stayed with the Riaños at Toledo, and went back there again and again. He crossed the Sierra de Guadarrama on foot for the first time in the summer of 1883; and to the Sierra, as to Toledo, he returned continually, above all in winter, spring and autumn. "Francisco Giner", as Julián Besteiro said at the dedication of the "Geologists' Well" many years afterwards, "wandered over these mountains with a handful of small boys in search of the Spain of the future."

In summer he usually went to the north. First it was to the Montaña of Santander, to the home of his friend Linares; and from there he made many excursions on foot in the western part of the province. "He was particularly fond of San Vicente de la Barquera", Sr Cossío tells us. "The place is a romantic blend, in harmony with his own character, of history, art, ruins and decayed manor houses, with an absence alike of pretentious *parvenus* and middle class vulgarity;—a ruined castle on a hill, reflected in the obscure tranquillity of an estuary smooth as a lake; a wide stretch of beach without bathing-establishments or bathing-huts; a splendid panorama of sea and mountain. There he was beloved by all; there he brought the Institution on its earliest excursions, and there the Society of old alumni of the Institution has built its house for summer colonies of poor children."

After 1891, Don Francisco spent his holidays in Galicia, his refuge being a house and garden near Betanzos, "belonging to the family of the disciple whose home was likewise his own". He enjoyed the isolation and retirement; "he made friends with the poorest villager, and with all the trees in the garden". There he wrote the essays which belong to the last period of his life; and from there he set out for long tramps along the coast. Latterly he became more devoted than ever to the Castilian sierras; and he died dreaming of the life of a hermit, in a hut belonging to the Institution at Navacerrada, though his sociable disposition would have made it impossible for him to live for long away from his friends and disciples.

"It is impossible", a friend has remarked, "to explain to those who never knew him what Don Francisco was like in the country. He seemed to draw out of natural objects all the divinity that was in them." When he was in the country he preferred not to talk. He did not usually work there, or even read. Nature absorbed him completely. "Sometimes he ran about like a child, or lay down in the sun, or walked 20 to 25 miles a day, even when he was over seventy; in winter he would bathe in the icy water of the mountain streams." In the country Don Francisco felt himself to be in the presence of God. "How he must have suffered", Sr de Zulueta wrote, at the time of his death, "at having to leave the Church, tearing himself away from the community of his people and their tradition! He did all he could to avoid it. As a young Krausist thinker, he heard mass on Sundays; and preserved, like his friend Fernando de Castro,[1] the hope of a reform of the church of Spain." That hope, like so many others in the world of religion, vanished after the decision of the Vatican council and Pio Nono's "Syllabus" of 1864. Catholicism, as practised in Spain, was too dishonest for Don Francisco. He considered that it was not right, that it would be sheer hypocrisy, for him to go on calling himself a Catholic. A Christian, yes, but not a member of the Church of Rome. It seemed to him cowardice to deliver himself up, without a struggle, to a ready-made doctrinal solution.[2] Once outside the established Church, his religious feelings became purer and more intense. He always spoke of the Catholic Church with respect, even though it was a Church which would prevent him from being buried next to his own mother. Wherever he was, he was in the presence of God. "But sometimes he would go into a lonely church, a forgotten wayside chapel, perhaps seeking an emotion that was purely aesthetic, perhaps led by the idea that it might, after all, some day be possible to pour new wine into the old bottles."[3] What would he have said to the neo-Catholic arguments of to-day? The argument of an English convert: "That's mere emotion!

[1] See page 43.   [2] Pijoán, 79.
[3] Zulueta, *Boletín* (1915), 47.

It should be a business proposition; and your business is to save your own soul". Or this—the argument of a Spanish Jesuit, repeated by a Spanish professor in England: "You say that Spanish priests do not wash, do not change their clothes as often as they might. Do you mind whether the clerk in the booking office washes, or changes his clothes? What is important for you is that he should give you the right ticket to Spain; and so with a priest, that he should give you the right ticket to Heaven". What would Don Francisco have said to such arguments? It is unlikely that he would have recognized them as arguments at all. The first he would have thought unworthy of anyone living in England—the England that *he* knew; and as for the second, Don Francisco had a clean shirt every day. "I don't like one or two silk shirts," he once said to a student. "I prefer a dozen cotton ones."

Don Francisco's private life was as transparent as his life in public. He always lived *en famille*; there was nothing more opposed to his character than the isolation of the celibate, a room in an hotel, or the cell of a holy hermit. He always needed a hearth, *un hogar* (he preferred the English word "home") with "the gentle contrasts of female society and filial tenderness, with the romping of young people and the perpetual din and clatter of small children", and in the midst of all this he did his day's work. He had his favourite pupils, of course; each new one seemed for a short time to be more wonderful than all the rest. But by temperament Don Francisco was essentially a family man. "And thus", Sr Cossío writes, "though the hopes were frustrated which he had once cherished of founding a 'home' for himself, he preserved in his heart, all through his life, the sacred cult of that impossible thing, and succeeded in making a 'home' in the home of another—it was really his—a position of a true father and grandfather, achieving the happiness of living and dying as he would have liked, surrounded by children and grandchildren." It is said that he once had a *novia*; but her parents objected to the idea of marrying anyone as revolutionary as Don Francisco. However, the pair began to write letters to each other again later in life, and Don Francisco must have felt as Mr Thomas Holbrook would have felt, if he ever received a letter from Miss Matty—*Cranford* was a well-known book in that household.

Don Francisco was a very little man; it was one of the most striking things about him, for most of his friends were of average height and some of them—Azcárate, Salmerón, Uña, for instance, were noticeably taller than their fellows. "He had a wiry little body, which (like his mind) was in perpetual motion, crowned by a large, noble head with a slightly long face, and brown eyes which were by turns an extraordinary mixture of kindness and ferocity. He had a short, pointed beard which was thick and stiff, and white from his fortieth year. As a whole, in form and colour he reminded one of the saints painted by Ribera, were it not for the restless energy of his movements."[1]

He was like a living statue of himself, a statue of earth, air, fire and water. To such an extent had he freed himself from the dross of daily life, that when speaking to him you thought that you were speaking to his image, which had come back to earth, true to life and everlasting. Yes; you would have said that he was never going to die now; that he had already passed through death without anyone knowing it, and that he was with us, as a spirit for ever and ever.[2]

It was in the garden of the Institution (Sr de Zulueta thinks) that he reached the plenitude of his activity, walking up and down, talking to some friend, passing in and out among the groups of boys and girls who were playing there.

In the sunshine, his bald head and bronzed face stood out as in a photographic negative against the whiteness of his hair and beard.

"He would suddenly cut short the conversation to say something to a small boy who ran past: and then pick up the thread of his discourse, or change the subject, speaking now in a tone of intimacy, now in more elevated language, and often both at once."

He often spoke of the Institution, what it was and what it signified. One day some visitors arrived: two foreign teachers

[1] Cossí *Boletín* (1915), 37.   [2] Juan Ramón Jiménez, *Boletín* (1915).

whom Don Francisco showed over the house and took into the class-rooms. This was how he humbly summed up his judgment on the value of his work:

Here you will see nothing really worth looking at. The garden is small; the place second-rate. We have nothing much in the way of laboratories or a library. Even the teaching does not often satisfy us. It is a pity.... But you will say: "How can persons who appear to be honest men devote their lives to a centre of education, when they are convinced of its defects?" Well...like this. We have here one thing which seems to us good, and, as far as it goes, excellent. One thing only: an aim.[1]

During his last two summer holidays Don Francisco yielded to the persuasion of his friends, and began to make a selection from his old articles on education. In the summer of 1913, first in the Casilla de la Sierra (in the mountains near Madrid), and then at San Vitorio near Betanzos, he began the work of revision; in October, the "perpetual motion of his mind" grew more intense as the moment came to give his ideas their final form. Yet notes and slips of paper dated November, 1913, in spite of being daily within his reach and sometimes by his bedside, remained incomplete at the time of his death; although a half sheet, written doubtless in the last months of his life, begins "I should like to leave the book of education articles finished, with the additions".

"Two problems tormented him" (Sr Cossío writes in the introduction to the book published after Don Francisco's death in 1915),[2] "both of them concerned with the Institution and the educational work into which he had put his whole heart." One was the progress of the Institution during the forty years of its existence; the other was the question of religious instruction in schools; and he came forward for the last time to show in the clearest possible light how religious education without dogma is, and always should be, a fountain of peace in the school—"in the true school which joins men together and generates a feeling of brotherhood between them".

[1] Luis de Zulueta, *Boletín* (1915), 52.
[2] Giner de los Ríos, *Ensayos de Educación* (Ediciones de La Lectura).

Here are some of the earliest rough notes, the first sketch hardly outlined, of what he meant to have written:

1. Religion is neither an infirmity nor a passing phenomenon of history, like war or slavery, but a permanent spiritual function which the school should educate.

2. By no means confessionally, that is to say presenting no confession as [the only one] worthy of faith.

3. Should be taught culturally, as [we] teach the history of the Hebrew people and the contents of the Old Testament, the history of Christianity....

4. Putting into it all respect and courteous consideration, not merely negative, but positive, *i.e.* according to the spirit of the Chicago Congress.

5. Avoiding comparative judgments.

6. The main thing is that this should be done in all the things which cause division. The school is not for that. In Europe to-day, the problems of politics, economics and religion are those which excite most passion. So they should be explained objectively, and no more. The school exists, not to divide but to create. Take care, in dealing with children: (*a*) not to profane their love, open to everything; (*b*) not to anticipate judgments which they cannot make for themselves. So it is repugnant to make them take part in disputed questions, *e.g.* signing protests for or against the Republic, the Monarchy, the temporal or spiritual power of the Pope, or rationalism, catholicism, protestantism; or the liberal, conservative or labour parties....Nor take them to meetings, including those for the liberty of conscience or neutrality of the school (what do they know about that!), with the abuse and profanation of little creatures who ought to be educated in reserve and love, "cum magna reverentia".

7. The State should endeavour to suppress this kind of confessional or political instruction. Common sense condemns schools which are monarchist, republican, catholic, etc. But not religious and political education (citizenship).

*   *   *

It remains for others to reckon up the balance of what we have won and lost, done and failed to do....The successes are, after all, superficial, apparent; the failures, for us, clear and profound; and no doubt the part most useful and helpful to us. If only the remedies were too!

★   ★   ★

We cry out to the four winds of heaven without hatred of anyone, neither the Jesuits, nor the Masons, catholics, protestants, atheists... but against the loafers (*haraganes*) whether they are republicans, liberals, conservatives or Carlists—all who shrug their shoulders at the idea of popular education and the interests of culture.

★   ★   ★

Our anxiety will always be: to avoid war, barbarism, savage intolerance, Africanism; to work in peace and harmony with all the world, in the endless problems, technical or spiritual, common to all, whether we like it or not—allowing ourselves to be attacked without replying, and even, as a rule, without protest, without defence; and all that without disdain, considering that it is as natural in them as it would be inconceivable in us.

Other notes were concerned with the training of teachers; "the difficulty of bringing the profession of elementary schoolmaster within the horizon of the middle-classes". But that was "just where the Institution came in"; university men should be brought to the elementary schools. The highly cultivated schoolmaster, the man of high moral training, should be sent as a missionary to the fields and villages of Spain.

The spirit of Don Francisco Giner de los Ríos lives on in the Institution, the *Institución Libre de Enseñanza*, and in the schools and colleges derived from it; above all in the great secondary school at Madrid, the *Instituto-Escuela*, and the university college, the *Residencia de Estudiantes*. His main object was to make men—a work that was slow but sure: *La obra lenta pero segura*, as he called it.

"Oh, this Spain, this Spain!" Don Francisco exclaimed one day, "what is to happen to it? The best men die without leaving any to come after them, or produce only one generation of intelligent men —three or four generations at the most—and you have to begin all over again every twenty years. If we could only profit by all we have already! But we are so divided between Catholics and

Liberals, that the one half of us cannot profit by what the other half knows and does."[1]

The work has been slow, but it has also been sure. Scattered over Spain and Spanish America there are thousands of men who, directly or indirectly, have gained something from Don Francisco. And when, in 1931, there was a need for men, to take charge and sacrifice themselves for the good of the country, those who had been at the Institution were not lacking. The pity of it is that there were not more of them. An "Institutionist" like Don Julián Besteiro, not only in the Speaker's chair in the Cortes but in every town and village council in Spain, would have saved the Second Republic from just those slips of which its enemies, particularly in England, have made so much.

[1] Pijoán, 58–9.

VII

DON FRANCISCO GINER (4)
The Borderland of Law and Ethics

LAW

DON FRANCISCO GINER was for more than thirty years professor of the Philosophy of Law at the University of Madrid. Students have often related (as in the last chapter) what it was like to go to his lectures; but what were they about? What did he understand by the philosophy of law? The subject was one which Don Francisco regarded as peculiarly his own. His method, although it underwent slight modification as the years went by and was adapted to the changing conditions of contemporary life, was always inspired by the philosophy of Krause, introduced into Spain (as has been shown in Chapter III) in the fifties and sixties of the last century. The position may be indicated by saying that it consists in giving to law an ethical content greater than that assigned to it by other systems, to the point, even, of suppressing so characteristic a feature of law as coercion.

Though he never wrote his lectures down, Don Francisco Giner and his pupil Alfredo Calderón (1850–1907) published an introduction to the subject, in which every sentence seems as if it had come straight out of one of those boxes of notes, hastily scribbled in a microscopic handwriting on half sheets of notepaper and the backs of old envelopes—notes which are so difficult to read that an expert disciple is necessary to interpret them, and so full of ideas that they would provide enough material for several generations of researchers.[1] The teaching which he pursued with such tenacious enthusiasm was carried on in spite of the hostility of many of his colleagues; and his lectures were given "in semi-darkness, in the inhospitable lecture-theatre of that barrack of a university".

[1] Castillejo, in introduction to *Resumen de la Filosofía del Derecho*, by Francisco Giner and Alfredo Calderón.

His mind (Sr Castillejo observes) was a distinctly Southern mind, and his thoughts were illuminated and given clear outline by his words. The thoughts were often too complex or too tentative to dare show themselves without the feeling of urgency imparted by the lecture-room. Yet when they appeared under those conditions, they were already cut and polished by having rubbed up against other intelligences and the fresh young brains of his pupils. His philosophy started from common knowledge, and his law from the consciousness of the people itself. Knowledge, for Don Francisco, was a social product, the lecture-room a laboratory, and teaching the result of collaboration and joint effort.

Yet from the outset he was faced by a difficulty of definition: what exactly was meant by the philosophy of law, *filosofía del derecho*? The difficulty is increased for us by the fact that in Spanish (as in French and German) the one word *derecho* (*droit, Recht*) has to do duty for both "law" and "right". It is (as Maitland said) never quite our "right" and never quite our "law". The philosophy of law (or right) as expounded by Don Francisco Giner did not include all law, or law considered historically; it was concerned rather with the theory of law in its relation to the State. He endeavoured to distinguish what was eternal from what was temporary, what was permanent from what depended on man. Law (or right), in the opinion of Don Francisco, as of Krause, was a part of eternal truth; and in so far as every thought of eternal truth is called an "idea" or a "concept", it might be said that the object of the philosophy of law was the study of the idea of Right. In order that this idea of Right may bear fruit, it must take some practical form, "some concrete type of practical realization".[1]

Don Francisco would point out how (according to Plato) justice was not founded on the bad disposition of man, but on his good and human qualities. He would remind his audience of the myth of how justice came to earth. The compassion of the gods before the mutual strife of mortals moved them to grant to man a share in their divine nature, and so it happened

---

[1] Fernando de los Ríos, *La Filosofía del Derecho en Don Francisco Giner*, 30.

that they granted to each and every one the sense of justice. So
it was not from something which contradicts the divine—from
sin—that law, or right, or justice proceeds, nor yet from the
limitation of man's actions, but from Divinity itself and from
the vision of the perfect man.

For Don Francisco, there were two different spheres in which
law (or right) could exist: one was intimate and interior,
"immanent", and the other transitive, exterior, social. The
second sphere is generally recognized; it represents the social
environment in which there are various persons, or "subjects";
and agreement, "a concordance of wills", is necessary so that
these wills may be called upon when they are needed. But there
are cases in which this relation is found within one and the
same individual; and in that case the legal, "juristic" relationship still exists within the same "subject".

We know (he would say) that there is an 'immanent' law dwelling
in our inmost being; for the legal relationship has two possible
positions: that of plaintiff and that of defendant, but it does not need
two separate persons. Thus I may be plaintiff against myself but a
defendant in my own case....If I am to fulfil my destiny, I must seek
the conditions which favour it and avoid those which prevent its
achievement—such, for instance, as the irrational destruction of my
property, the abuse of my faculties, the contempt of my will or the
dissipation of my goods.

The real fount of justice is something which everyone should have
within himself.

This (Don Francisco admitted) is the voice of a minority;
but it is, nevertheless, the basis of the Spanish school of legal
philosophy. At the root of the system is the self, offered in its
most intimate moments as *action*; and this conception of the life
of the spirit as a world of actions gives a certain originality to
the doctrine of this school on the relation of law to morality.

Law, like morality, embraces all acts which have any
reference to the rational end in view. The problem of both is the
Good, and the difference between them depends on the manner
in which they are regarded. We might say that, taken together,
they form Ethics and constitute its two main directions.

An act may be materially good and yet morally bad, either through lack of purity of motive, or because the reason for the act is opposed to the nature of the act itself.[1] To forgive a debt to one who has fallen upon evil days, for example, is an act which, superficially considered, is good. But (we may ask), for what reason was the debt forgiven? Is it a matter of indifference, in judging the moral position of the "subject", to understand his surroundings and his motives at the time the debt was forgiven and consider whether the act was committed through desire of vainglory, for social prestige, or to satisfy the pressing summons of a sense of duty? Morality does not consist in the specific content of an action but in its relation to the state of mind of the person who performs it. In whatever we do (he concluded) we should have, as our only motive, the intrinsic kindliness of the act which we perform.[2]

These are examples of the way in which Don Francisco would choose his theme from "the borderland where ethical speculation marches with jurisprudence". There was another problem of a more speculative sort which also interested him profoundly: the "group-personality", or *persona social*. This requires an explanation. Besides men or "natural persons", the actual law of most countries knows persons of another kind. In particular it knows the corporation, and for many purposes it treats the corporation much as it treats a man or a woman. Like a man or a woman, the corporation has rights and also duties.[3] In the eye of the law, a corporation is a person, not a "natural person", but (according to modern legal systems) a fictitious, artificial, juristic person; a "group" personality. The fictitious person must not be confused with the natural persons which compose it. It is capable of owning things, of possessing "proprietary rights"; but, unlike a "natural" person, it is incapable of "knowing, intending, willing, acting" (except through agents), just as it is incapable (even by its agents) of marrying and giving in marriage.

[1] "Formal Right [or Law] might be material Unright, and formal Unright might be material Right" (Maitland).
[2] F. de los Ríos, *La Filosofía del Derecho en Don Francisco Giner* (1916), 126–7.   [3] F. W. Maitland, *Collected Papers*, III, 304 ff.

The group-personality was described by Don Francisco as being formed

by the union of individuals who achieve something in common by their organic co-operation, sometimes instinctively, sometimes deliberately. There may be a single end in view, or many; but with these conditions they form a true personality which has its own reality, its own unity and its own spirit—the family feeling, the spirit of a corporation, public opinion, etc.—its own corporate strength and means of action.[1]

Two questions of capital importance to the group-personality were discussed by Don Francisco Giner: the nature of the legal act which brings it to birth, and the question of its reality. Don Francisco's conclusions agree on both these points with Gierke and Maitland.[2] In his work on *La Persona Social*, Giner develops the hypothesis which he had before merely indicated: the principle of contract was not enough to explain something so essentially distinct from it as the corporation. He had already pointed this out in his *Principles of Natural Law* (1873) and his *Juristic and Political Studies* (1875). Contract, he said, rested on the fact that a number of individuals took part in it without any real unity being established between them, or a new "person" being formed. The group-personality, on the contrary, so far from maintaining the separate and independent existence of its members, maintained the independence of the whole body.[3] Maitland put the matter in a nutshell: If n men unite themselves in an organized body, the law must see $n + 1$ persons.[4]

In the Middle Ages, each "social organism"—it is safer to avoid the word "state" at that period—was a congeries of rudimentary corporate bodies: township, county, guild, uni-

[1] F. de los Ríos, *La Filosofía del Derecho en Don Francisco Giner* (1916), 154–5.

[2] *Political Theories of the Middle Age*, by Dr Otto Gierke. Translated with an introduction by F. W. Maitland (Cambridge, 1900). Gierke's first published writings on the subject date from 1868.

[3] F. de los Ríos, *La Filosofía del Derecho en Don Francisco Giner* (1916), 155–6.

[4] *Collected Papers*, III, 316.

versity, etc. It is important to realize (for the histories of Spain do not usually make the point as clear as they might) that these bodies were not created by the kings. They came into existence in various ways; and then, being already in existence, applied to the king or lord for protection and privileges, which were set down in writing as "charters"—in Spanish, *fueros*. In medieval Spain there were on the one hand the groups of free population (*behetrías*) which, for greater safety, sought the protection of a powerful noble,[1] and, on the other, the townships (*villas*) which arose in places conquered from the Muslims. To encourage the inhabitants living in waste land and in exposed and dangerous situations, the kings granted them privileges such as personal freedom, remission of taxes, self-government or the recognition of such judicial practices as had already become customary. In such townships the slaves were freed, and a middle class developed industry and commerce, while the liberties of the township were guaranteed by a document—the charter (or *fuero*) granted by the king.

The growth of commerce and industry in these towns gave rise, from 1200 onwards, to the formation of professional trade guilds, *gremios*, and also to semi-civil, semi-religious corporate bodies, constituted by men of all classes for charitable or other non-professional objects, and known as *cofradías*. These bodies were "collective juristic persons". They formed real moral entities with an *esprit de corps* of their own, with a common house or hall, property both in money and land, a seal, a banner and a patron saint, the image of whom was carried (and is still carried on certain occasions) in solemn procession through the streets. Created as they were in the shadow of the municipalities, and favoured by the liberties and privileges which these already possessed, the guilds and *cofradías* rapidly increased in number and importance, claimed from the kings exceptional honours and privileges, and formed social bodies of great weight in the medieval Spanish cities. We must be clear, however, that guild charters did not create guilds, but granted them privileges once they had come into existence, amongst

[1] Altamira, *Historia de España y de la Civilización Española*, I, 516.

others those of exclusive trading rights, apprenticeship, the holding of land, etc.

At the close of the Middle Ages this form of organization began to disappear. Its disappearance was due to the dominance of Roman law which regarded all corporations as "fictitious persons" created by the State. A great canon-lawyer, Pope Innocent IV, first gave this conception currency in Europe; and on this basis all entities were dethroned and obliterated, if they intervened between the individual citizen and the despot king or sovereign state. This is the true explanation of the rebellion of the *Comuneros* of Castille, in the sixteenth century. That rising was ultimately a rising in defence of the *fueros*, the rights granted by the king to ancient groups which had not been created by him. These rights had become the bulwark of the existence of such groups. The attempt to suppress them was really an attack on those groups with the object of suppressing everything that intervened between the individual citizen and the unitary state. The two conceptions—group-personality and state-absolutism—were never so plainly (though unconsciously) engaged in conflict, as on this occasion in Spain.

From the seventeenth century onwards the king began to create corporations by Royal Charter, not merely to give them powers and privileges. By the nineteenth century, corporate organization had become so useful for trading purposes that the old methods of obtaining incorporation by Royal Charter or special Act of Parliament were found to be too cumbrous, and simpler methods of incorporation by the State were introduced.

Conditions in England differed materially from conditions in Spain, as Francisco Giner was well aware. In England, Roman law was never "received" as it was in Spain; but at the close of the Middle Ages a unitary state was formed, and mediatory corporate bodies were gradually obliterated, as elsewhere. But at the same time, the exclusively English idea of a *trust* was being established, and enforced in England by the Courts of Chancery; and this enabled a degree of corporate (or pseudo-corporate) life to persist in England to an extent which was impossible elsewhere, but which was essentially different from the corporate life of the Middle Ages. Behind a "screen" of trustees (as Maitland put it) all manner of groups can flourish in England: Lincoln's Inn, Lloyd's, the Stock Exchange, the Jockey Club, the whole Presbyterian system, "or even the Church of Rome with the Pope at its head"; for in the eye of the law of England, the Church of Rome is in the same position as a football club, much as that fact has surprised learned continental jurists.[1] In Spain, no such convenient shelter has been provided for "unincorporate bodies", such as the religious orders. The legal position of those orders in Spain is not well understood in this country, and our unfamiliarity with Spanish conditions has led to much misrepresentation. (See note on p. 145, Chapter VIII.)

From the theory of group-personality, Giner passed to the theory of the State. The description "State" (he said) belongs to as many "persons" as direct in a substantive manner a sphere of juristic activity, whether their "personality" is individual or social, natural or fictitious. The use of the word "person" and not "subject of proprietary rights" had, he pointed out, an essential value when applied to the State; because a State is what it is, not because it is subject to claims or rights, but because it is liable to obligations and services.

Consequently the State is not, as is generally thought—least of all the Social State, the Social organization of legal obligations—an order of authority, supremacy or power, but one of obligation and service to the rational purposes of life.[2]

POLITICS

In politics Don Francisco Giner took no active part. That is to say, he took no direct part; but there was hardly a generous measure of liberal reform among the few carried out in the repressive age of the restoration (from 1875 until his death in 1915) which did not owe something to his influence. The Restoration seemed to have, as its principal object, "the inocu-

[1] Maitland, *Collected Papers*, III, 364.
[2] F. de los Ríos, *La Filosofía del Derecho en Don Francisco Giner* (1916), 182.

lation with anaemia of all the politics and politicians in the country". Yet politicians would come to him quietly and un-ostentatiously for advice; for Don Francisco (though he some-times let people feel the rough side of his tongue) was both ready and willing to help anyone who needed his help and would come and explain his difficulties.

Though the best of Giner was in his conversation, his books also made their effect. Once more he collaborated with Alfredo Calderón, the pupil who helped him to put together the *Summary of the Philosophy of Law*, and the result was the *Principles of Natural Law*, "a little book, but a great revelation", especially for the generations who were studying law between 1873 and 1883. "It revealed to us (an undergraduate of that time has recorded) an idea that was rich, fertile and inex-haustible, besides being intensely human and full of the stuff of idealism and moral inspiration."[1] Even the Restoration con-stitution of 1876 was influenced by Giner's *Principles*; and the book contained in addition a special theory of political auto-nomism,—a notable improvement upon the abstract federalism, preached by Pi y Margall, which had proved so disastrous when put into practice during the First Republic.

There were also in the book ideas "which (says the author of the introduction to the latest edition) I should like to call ultra-European in this semi-African country, ideas which in a most unexpected and happy manner raised the status of Spain in the eyes of educated people in civilized countries, though they must have been almost unintelligible to anyone not born in England". They were ideas of peace, harmony and tolerance, leading to fruitful and generous co-operation in life and govern-ment, so that men of diametrically opposite opinions could smooth over their personal asperities and work together in complicated and delicate negotiations. The value of the book was not confined to Spain, as is shown by the German translation which appeared in 1907 under the title of *Zur Vorschule des Rechts* (Leipzig). The number of modern Spanish books which have been translated into German is limited.

[1] Giner, *Obras*, vol. I, Introduction.

The political ideals of Don Francisco Giner have been summarized from notes and conversations by Fernando de los Ríos, to whose little book, *La Filosofía del Derecho en Don Francisco Giner*, this chapter is greatly indebted. His views on democracy are of considerable interest at the present time, when the whole democratic view is being called in question. Nothing (he says) could be more opposed to the ideal of the Master than the indiscriminate application of the democratic principle to the whole of political life. We must proceed to analyse it scientifically; we must distinguish between *functions* in the State and *organs*. What to-day is called democracy was, in his eyes, the deliberate organization of the instruments of government, such as the electoral body; and since these are organs of the State, they can never include the whole of the people, nor is there any reason for desiring that they should do so. For there are functions of the life of the State which are purely technical, and which therefore only the technically equipped either can or ought to perform. When, in Spain, liberalism and democracy were united in such a way that the future of both seemed indissoluble, Don Francisco was one of the few who were heard to point out that the union was contrary to Right; and that what was called democracy was not a way of making the people share in the government, but of entrusting that share to a more or less numerous group; and that it was not the masses, nor the educated, but only the technically or scientifically trained who should be called upon, on occasions, "to find the necessary formula". This was the starting-point of his criticism of existing democracies, which depend on an appeal to the majority. The principle of the will of the majority has on occasions, no doubt, its justification; but it has little sense when the decision rests with science, or when science becomes the authority for the agreements which are concluded.

There was, even in the lifetime of Don Francisco, a feeling of protest in some of the more adventurous and objective spirits— a protest against parliamentary democracy, as being a régime of incompetence. This protest had nothing to do with Fascism, which had not been invented at the time of Don Francisco's

death in 1915. The protest to which he referred came from the
"left"; it was a characteristic development of trade unionism
and syndicalism, and it claimed that decisive power should
belong to "a capacitated minority". Don Francisco made two
observations on this doctrine. It was impossible (he said) to
construct a social body without paying attention to anything
more than its professional functions; while the legal control of
trade unions must be less the result of stern discipline than a work
of conviction and education.

Yet trade unionism implied certain positions which Don
Francisco shared with heart and soul: that every man must have
some trade or profession, and that the functions of government
—these being understood as the deliberate, intentional, reflective (or, as Don Francisco used to say, "artistic") functions
—need an adequate cultural preparation. For this reason, he
was not a friend of the jury system (which has never worked
well in Latin countries). But his hopes were raised by something else, which had in fact been accomplished by the Portuguese Republic, a thing which certain elements had endeavoured
to bring about in Spain also: the removal of some ministers
altogether from political action, so as to convert them into
permanent technical advisers. The root idea of Don Francisco in
regard to this problem lay in a theory he had of the special ends
and objects of life, the realization of which would demand
societies specialized in the performance of these objects. It was
in his conversation rather than in his writings that he developed
this idea, but suggestions of it may be found now and again in
his published works.[1]

By saying that the object of the State is to fulfil law (and
right)—that is to say that "every person should serve the object
of his life with every means at his disposal" without interfering
with other persons—Don Francisco stated the two phases of
liberalism: the necessity for tenacious action directed towards
the realization of the object of human existence, and the respect
for the feelings, the conscience, of everyone else. He had a

[1] *E.g. Estudios jurídicos y políticos* (La política antigua y la política nueva)
and *La Persona Social*, 191 and 295.

particular aversion from anything like compulsion, and his *Summary of the Philosophy of Law* contains a reasoned and powerful defence of voluntary service as against conscription.[1]

The respect which Don Francisco had for a high standard of conduct separated him from any man or party inclined to persecution or dictatorial measures; even the punishment of a criminal "had no justification in his eyes other than the necessity which the criminal had of it himself". From this, too, came his idea of the non-confessional school. "Take care (he said), when dealing with a child, not to profane his love for anything, and not to anticipate judgments which he cannot make for himself."[2]

The attitude adopted by Don Francisco was new in Spain and indeed in other countries; since the War, it has receded still farther from the realm of practical politics. For "the politics of the present are founded on a system of authority, whether under avowed dictatorships, or systems which still call themselves democratic; while the ideal of the Master was founded in the depths of the individual consciousness. The ideas prevailing to-day derive their support, on the one hand from the Penal Code, from fear, and on the other from a sentimental or religious abstraction: patriotism, the State. Those for which Don Francisco planned so resolutely were based on the cordial adhesion of individual members. The system under which we live is inorganic and doctrinaire; the one which he expounded is living and organic, founded upon competence, aptitude, fitness. It does not consider the main problem to be one of organization, but of action,—of what to do now, and what to do next". His policy was one of moderation, but it was practical. No one could speak more bitterly than Don Francisco of present social and economic conditions; but when he set his thoughts on a future which might have been (and might still be) an age of greater justice and nobility, he saw with satisfaction that the way thither was already pointed by co-operation and collectivism; the voluntary and spontaneous effort of a number

---

[1] *Resumen de la Filosofía del Derecho*, 251.
[2] *Ensayos de Educación*, prologue, xi.

of individuals for their mutual profit; and while he hailed with joy anything which seemed to signify the disappearance, improvement, or gradual replacement of the present political and economic system, he looked with aversion and profound misgiving on every organization of a disciplinary type.

Was not this attitude (it may fairly be asked) characteristic of the social politics derived from the legal philosophy of Krause? It is irrelevant to urge that the philosophy of Krause is out of date, that it was hopelessly muddle-headed, that, rejected by Germany, it found its only refuge in Spain. The vigour with which Krausism was attacked by ultramontane writers shows that there must have been something in it, something considered dangerous to obscurantism and authority. "There are books (Unamuno has remarked) of which not a single statement is left standing, and yet they have been books which led men to a large number of discoveries. Everything depends on that—on the feelings which an author arouses in others, even if it be by contradiction." This was never more true than of the works of Krause and Sanz del Río, which now seem definitely to belong to another age. But the originality of thought in Don Francisco Giner is still of to-day, depending as it does on its profound liberalism, and its being directed at the same time towards the humanist socialism afterwards expounded by his nephew, Fernando de los Ríos.[1]

The interest once taken in legal forms for their own sake—forms which were expected to bear fruit from their own virtue—has been transferred to man and his formation as a whole: to his inner disposition, to the width of his horizon, to the purification and amplification of his spirit, to the intensification of his energy.... All the rest: constitutions, laws, decrees—the "imperatives" in fact—are either new creations or historical remains of past conditions—means which only have value so far as they still contribute to the ends for which they were intended. What we all want nowadays are not new electoral laws, but electors with fresh minds; not a further reorganization of government-offices and courts of law, but better officials and better magistrates.[2]

[1] *El Sentido humanista del socialismo* (Madrid, 1925).
[2] *La Filosofía del Derecho en Don Francisco Giner*, 220–1.

EDUCATION

Those electors with fresh minds, those officials and magistrates who should be better public servants, could only be produced in one way—by better education. It should be sufficient condemnation of the educational practices which prevailed in Spain from the Restoration of 1875 to the republic of 1931, that those practices could produce only inattention and unpunctuality: royalists who were too late to defend their King, catholics who were too late to defend their Church and republicans whose divisions amongst themselves may one day make them too late to defend their Republic.

Spanish education as controlled by the religious orders should stand condemned for all time, on the results of 1875–1931; yet the restoration of that system of education may truly be described in the old electioneering phrase as the "first constructive plank" of the opposition platform. That is the system which English newspapers support when they heap ridicule on the republic, a system as far removed from English ideals as any educational system well could be; and a new "restoration" in Spain, which is sometimes vaguely and idly talked of in England, would mean not necessarily a restoration of the monarchy but a restoration of the dictatorship with unrestricted control of education by the religious orders.

It has frequently been stated that the republic, in denying complete liberty of education to the orders, is denying its own liberal principles. That, however, is not the case, as Don Francisco Giner would have been the first to point out. Don Antonio Zozaya, one of the older generation of those who were educated at the Free Institution, has taken up this point. It is (he says) an example of the eternal struggle between the two rival bands: those who confide everything to the State, and those who yield everything to the individual; the fight between those who assume that the subject has no rights whatever, and those who affirm that he has all rights. Are not both in the wrong? (he asks). To lack liberty is odious and unjust; but to claim it in everything is erroneous and absurd. Just as individuals have inalienable rights which the State cannot disregard or violate, so the State has a sphere of right of its own which it ought not to abandon to any individual, even though the whole nation, by means of universal suffrage, may vote against it. One of these rights of the State, which is at the same time a duty, is that of education. On this account, not even liberals can admit the absolute liberty of education, any more than they can countenance, in individual citizens, a liberty to declare war, to fix the amount of taxation or to control foreign relations. All these belong to the province of the central government— subject, of course, to such inspection and sanction as the Constitution may determine. Education is a function of the State; and should not be given over either to congregations or private individuals. Bitter experience (the writer adds) shows that, in Spain, education cannot even be left in the hands of the municipalities. Neither the State nor the individual is in possession of all rights for itself; each has only those which are essential to the fulfilment of its own purpose. For this reason, then, there should be freedom of thought, of assembly, of association, of the press and of the ballot; but there cannot be absolute freedom of education.[1]

So much for the right to educate. The object of the education given should be (according to Don Francisco Giner) "to produce a personality such that it shall spontaneously comply with law". This is the point of contact between the Philosophy of Law and Education—a point which occupied much of the Master's attention. For him, the object of education was not, as most people thought, to impose a body of habits or pieces of knowledge from outside on to the child or man whom it was desired to educate; but to encourage the development of the total personality in each human being.

Rational beings should be something more than mechanical repeaters of what they learn.... They possess—and that is precisely why they are "rational"—a germ capable of independent growth. Side by side with the intelligence, in all its vigour, the other potentialities of the soul should gradually show themselves in their natural

---

[1] *La Sociedad contra el Estado*, 252.

ways: the love of beauty and of great things; the moral sense; the will, and above all the sane, virile, fertile sense which has delivered us from the limbo of animality where the child and the primitive man doze away their lives.[1]

Starting, then, from the conditions which the individual brings with him into this world, education has to raise us "to the plenitude of our being".

The education which Giner desired and achieved is not merely intellectualist; it bears also all the features of personalism, *i.e.* the spirit of action which was so characteristic of his thought. For him, the important thing was the personality as a whole.[2] The method of education should not be limited to instruction, the mere accumulation of knowledge in the mind; for the mind is not developed by that means. Nor should the method consist of a purely external educational mechanism; since it is useless "to think of substituting this mechanism for life, liberty and conscience". The true method should be rooted in the very life of the subject; and it is, in fact, none other than the so-called "intuitive" method in the widest sense—the method which, for abstractions, substitutes reality. This method demands that there shall be presented to the pupil "facts, data, individual and concrete forms upon which he can afterwards build his own conclusions". It also requires that the pupil, as far as he is capable, should think for himself.

This leads, in practice, to doing without text-books; as also to laboratory work and to excursions to factories, museums, historic towns, the country and foreign parts. "Personality" means activity, life; and to develop it, activity and life form the only method. The only way of learning to do things is to do them.

Most important of all is the education of the teacher himself; and since education is, in the last resort, the general raising of the level of human life, the teacher must be regarded as a species of lay missionary. One of the last notes scribbled by Don Francisco before his death was: "Train teachers, that is to say, missionaries".

[1] *Ensayos de Educación*, 119. [2] Viqueira, II, 459.

PHILOSOPHY

The philosophy of Giner, one of his pupils remarks, was influenced by all the living ideas of his age. He received inspiration from Spinoza, Kant and Rousseau; he gathered Hegel's feeling for unity and Schelling's synthesis of Nature and Spirit; he accepted from Savigny the gradual formation, in the popular consciousness, of ideas of law and right; he made use of the conquests of positivism, the sociology of Wundt, the idealist tendency of the theological school and the harmonious solidity of the system of Krause. Further, he owed something to the English educationists and the Spanish mystical tradition. "The dominant faculty in his mind was his aptitude for sifting and purifying ideals, as a lodestone attracts iron filings from the inert dust surrounding them."[1]

Don Francisco went on learning until within a few days of his death. In every book he found something worth underlining, worth remembering. A school of philosophy, in his view, was a direction, an orientation of thought; the fact that he considered certain positions to be essential did not always or necessarily mean that he took that point of view himself. In his lectures[2] he would explain how Greek philosophy divided the world into two orders which were substantive (*i.e.* having a separate and independent existence), and opposite: Nature and Law, φύσις and νόμος. This opposition between Nature and Law was affirmed and strengthened by Kant: Nature (in his system) meant cause. Opposed to it was culture, and this could only be interpreted by having recourse to a principle which denied all concomitance with the cause: the principle of Finality. The principle of causality sufficed for a scientific knowledge of the physical world, and everything exposed to its conditions; the principle of finality was indispensable for the acquisition of knowledge of what was unconditional: God, beauty and the world of ideas. Kant had said: "Act so that you always treat humanity, whether in yourself or another, as an end, not as a means". The opposi-

---

[1] Castillejo, *Minerva-Zeitschrift*, 207.
[2] F. de los Ríos, *La Filosofía del Derecho en Don Francisco Giner*, 42.

tion between these two principles could still be seen in many of the leaders of philosophic thought of the time; it was still the prevailing thesis.

But at all times (he would go on) there had existed a position of protest, a position which often consisted in taking Nature as the archetype, and denying that the two orders, cause and effect, had to remain separated. This attitude culminated in Spinoza. All things (Spinoza said) were nourished by one substance, and all that existed was only a manifestation of that single substance and of its two essential, internal "modalities" which he called *natura naturans* (that which is in itself and conceived through itself, *e.g.* God in so far as He is considered as a free cause) and *natura naturata* (everything which follows from the necessity of the nature of God, or of any one of God's attributes). The one single substance Spinoza called "Nature" or "God", and everything, according to his view, was determined *ex necessitate divinae naturae*.[1]

Then he would explain how, after the time of Kant, the philosophy of the Romantic period took up two distinct attitudes before Nature. For Fichte, Nature was an obstacle which the Spirit encountered in the course of its development. It was the "non-spiritual", and its value was chiefly negative—"chiefly", because the spirit, on meeting with that obstacle, turned inward on itself, and by this means acquired consciousness of itself and of the world. In Schelling, the place of Nature had become more important; it was not "the spiritual", but neither was it "the non-spiritual". Spirit and Nature were two manifestations of a primary Being, raised above the opposition of subject and object—a Being which signified the identity of the real and the ideal; the Absolute, or Nature as subject; Creative Nature. Krause had taken something from both Fichte and Schelling: the idea of the Absolute; and, nearer to Schelling than to Fichte, he saw in Nature and Spirit the Real and the Ideal, and in God, the principle common to both.

The somewhat obscure thought of Krause was the point of departure for Don Francisco himself; but it led him on to the

---

[1] *Ethics*, Part I, Prop. XXIX and Scholia.

position which he ultimately reached—the position which filled his life and excited his imagination, above all as an educator. Why say that Man and Humanity were synthetic expressions of the two states of Being, Spirit and Nature, and deny this to a bird, a plant or a stone? Nature, which some had tried to deprive of all spiritual meaning, was, considered in itself, in its laws and products, a particular sphere of the world, of divine creation, of universal energy.

Don Francisco's metaphysical problem was concerned with a conception of the world in which the two main directions of history, the pagan and the Christian, were united. Not "God and Nature", but "God in Nature and in the Spirit", as in two rays of light issuing from a common source.[1]

The philosophy of Krause had already shown a decided inclination towards practical problems, juristic and moral. In the same way the educational work of Francisco Giner was an aggregate of speculative results, a concrete application of theory to the struggles of our time.[2] Not that his philosophy (except his philosophy of law) was ever expressed by him in a system; it was scattered in his different works and in his letters, conversations and classes.[3] His whole thought was penetrated by the idea of action, of vital activity. The division between theory and practice (he held) was vain,

because basic principles, which appear to the uninstructed to be abstruse, fantastic and far removed from the realities of life, are precisely those which prove the most fertile, since they include all the rest in the infinite variety of their possible applications.[4]

Giner denied, also, that the only propulsive and creative agent was the intellect; he affirmed that intellect constituted only one aspect of the human spirit, and that, without the intimate warmth of personal unity, it did not possess any real value. Nature and Spirit were not higher or lower, but of the

[1] F. de los Ríos, *loc. cit.*
[2] Besteiro, *Boletín* (1915), 88.
[3] Viqueira, in Spanish edition of Vorländer's *History of Philosophy*, ii, 455.
[4] Giner, *Ensayos de Educación*, 107.

same category: each of those worlds produced what the other was prevented from producing.[1]

RELIGION

The religious spirit which penetrates the thought of Francisco Giner was "lived rather than worked out philosophically";[2] but it was none the less genuinely religious for all that.

The word "godless" is so freely applied nowadays to those whose religious beliefs, though not coinciding with an established dogma, are none the less deeply felt and sincere, that it is important to make as clear as possible what Don Francisco's religious beliefs really were. Something of his early religious development has been given in the previous chapter. In essence, religion meant for Don Francisco:

The sense of reverence, of serene emotion and sympathy (or charity)....

(Notice that he translates "charity" by "sympathy"—and why not? "Though I speak with the tongues of men and of angels and have not *sympathy...Sympathy* never faileth... Faith, hope and *sympathy*, but the greatest of these is *sympathy*.") sympathy, not only for things around us, but above all, veneration and love for the Source from which all this springs.

Religion is:

The formation of this spirit, both in the understanding and experience of life and in the accomplishment of its purposes with this intention; always becoming more instinctive, more delicate and profound as far as its culture allows. It is the permanent function of all education and therefore of every school.

In reality (he adds), "every grown man in the intimacy of his soul, [and in those regions which are] more or less clear and more or less profound and vague, where the light of reflexion does not always penetrate, and without perhaps knowing it himself—every man has his religion, as he has his politics, his aesthetics and his philosophy; formed all of them by the co-

---

[1] *Ensayos de Educación*, 237.   [2] Viqueira, *loc. cit.*

operation of permanent and historical forces of very different kinds ". No one (he declared) could live in any other way.

The results of all this inexhaustible energy are so deep, so multiform and so delicate, that it is impossible to point to each of them individually. We can recognize them in all those men who have been able to yield the best fruits of their spirit, thanks to their contact with the spirit of Giner; in all those institutions, public and private, which were created by men and women fired by the warmth of that heart; in an influence diffused through all educational, scientific and social reform, which has been translated into a raising of the moral and intellectual level of many people in Spain.

VIII

SALMERÓN

the Leader against his own leadership

O NE night, about 1860, Captain Nicolás Estévanez went
to a debate at the Ateneo. A debate at the Ateneo in
Madrid corresponds (as we have suggested before) to a
debate at the Union at Oxford or Cambridge. It is unwise to
give it more importance, or less. The motions are often as
startling as they are academic, but they have the virtue of
making members think before they speak, and the Ateneo de
Madrid has long been known as "a Holland of free speech".
Captain Estévanez was a good regimental officer, who, through
interest in the welfare of his men, had come to take a wider
interest in the welfare of mankind, particularly that portion of
mankind which existed in Spain under the full-skirted régime
of Isabella II. It was as natural for him to go to the Ateneo and
listen to the debates, as it was for him afterwards in a moment
of emergency to accept the civil governorship of Madrid,
being pulled out of bed by a republican Prime Minister at
2 o'clock in the morning and told to proceed to his office forthwith. In the most natural way, too, he composed his *Memoirs*,
which, delightful and valuable as they are for the history of the
period, have escaped the notice of most foreign and superficial
observers. Spanish memoirs, it is felt, should be the work of
men and women of title, and Estévanez was not even a general!

The *Memoirs* of Captain Nicolás Estévanez give us the first
public appearance of Salmerón:

Suddenly there stood up a young man of about 30; tall, thin, dark,
with large, prominent and expressive eyes. The chairman nodded,
but the meeting grew restive; there were murmurs of protest that
everyone had had enough, and that they were tired of oratory after
half a dozen long speeches....

The unknown orator, then, began under the most unfavourable
conditions; but the first phrases of his exordium were scarcely heard

before silence became general, and in a short time he was clearly speaking with the unanimous admiration of the public. It was Salmerón.

Although he was already famous in the university, the public at that time did not know him, nor did I. I confess I was astonished at his diction, his style and his gestures, which were not at all like those of most of our orators. But in spite of everything, I came away from that meeting in the belief that there would be a disaster with such rare eloquence, owing to the eclectic spirit of so philosophic a speaker. There was no way of getting out of him any definite declaration, or affirmation of republican principles, though he was as republican then as he is now (1899). He was trying, no doubt, to attract those social calamities, the neutrals, and those implacable enemies of democracy, the conservatives.[1]

Salmerón's father had been a country doctor at Alhama la Seca, about fifteen miles inland from the Mediterranean port of Almería. Almería was once a Moorish dockyard; and the name Alhama la Seca gives in three words the whole history of the place: the Moorish bath which in Christian times had been allowed to run dry. Salmerón's mother had been a Srta Alonso. He had a brother, twelve years older than himself, a lawyer who was a member of King Amadeo's government in 1872. It is a curious irony of national biography that the only other Salmerón to achieve eminence should have been one of the first disciples of Ignatius Loyola—Alonso de Salmerón; and a scholastic philosopher might deduce from the order of their names that the ultimate resting-place of the soul of Salmerón y Alonso, sometime President of the Spanish republic, would be the opposite of that of Alonso de Salmerón, the disciple of Ignatius Loyola.

Nicolás Salmerón y Alonso was born in 1838. He went to school at Almería and to the University of Granada, where he met Francisco Giner. He first became known in Madrid through his speeches at the Ateneo, and in 1864 he gained in competitive examination the chair of history in the University of Oviedo.

---

[1] Estévanez, *Fragmentos de mis memorias*, 2nd ed. (1903), 281–2.

Now Oviedo is a very long way from Madrid, in Asturias and almost within sight of the Bay of Biscay; and though its university has since come to be ranked, and deservedly, as one of the best in Spain—Azcárate used to say that the man who had been to Oviedo, even only for a couple of years, could go alone anywhere in the world—the prospects of a professorship there in the 'sixties were not alluring to a man who felt that he had a future. Salmerón remained in Madrid. History was not really his subject. He bided his time, reading Kant, speaking at the Ateneo, and interesting himself in education. Like many others, then and since, he concluded that what was most wrong with Spain was a system of education which allowed a virtual monopoly of teaching to the religious orders; men and women did not become trained teachers merely from the fact of residing in a religious house. Then there was the question of method. "Private education, the downtrodden slave of the official programme with its memorized texts and compulsory examinations", might, he thought, be replaced by an "international college" which should set education in new surroundings and place the child from his earliest years within the reach of free classes, like those in which men of real distinction and proved capacity were just then endeavouring to awake an interest in natural history, art, law, economics and history in small classes of grown men. All this happened before the "September Revolution", the end of the reign of Isabella II, and foreshadowed the "Free Institution" founded after the restoration by the friends of Don Francisco Giner.

A chair of philosophy became vacant in 1866. Salmerón's thoughts had first turned to philosophy in the lecture-room of Sanz del Río, to whose general feeling in ethics, law and social science Spanish thinkers of the day turned their attention from the most diverse points of view. Like Francisco Giner, Fernando de Castro, and Sanz del Río himself, Salmerón had to leave the university in 1867 through the persecutions of the egregious minister Orovio; but on the fall of the monarchy in the following year he was elected to the professorship of metaphysics, a post which he held—with one long interval—for the rest of his life. Salmerón, however, fared worse than Sanz del Río or Francisco Giner. He was a member of a secret democratic committee, and on that account was imprisoned for five months in 1867. The September revolution found him at Almería, much broken in health; but he returned to Madrid immediately as a member of the revolutionary *Junta*. He was a candidate for the Constituent Cortes of 1869, but was not elected until 1871. On the abdication of Amadeo he voted for a republic; and he was appointed Minister of Grace and Justice in the first republican cabinet.

"Here is Your Excellency's carriage", they said to him, as he left the ministry for the first time.

"I have neither carriage nor excellency", he replied.[1]

One of his first acts as minister was an order (20th February, 1873) putting an end to the change of law officers with every change of government; until then they had been the victims of interests which were not concerned with their judicial function, tossed hither and thither by those interests until they succumbed to the dead weight of the surrounding medium. The Spanish Bench owes to Salmerón the first recognition of its independence and its professional dignity.[2]

Four months later he was appointed President (Speaker) of the Cortes.

The republic of 1873 (as was suggested in a previous chapter) was represented in office by a group of persons of the most austere and respectable character which humanity is capable of producing. They came forward to serve their country with no thought of personal advantage; but their talent was speculative rather than administrative, and they lacked the necessary hold on the immediate realities of Spain. Even the critical spirit and moral fervour of Nicolás Salmerón, the most illustrious of the rulers of 1873, were more appropriate to the understanding and commentary of the *Republic* of Plato than to piloting safely into port the humble republic of Spain.[3]

[1] Altamira, *Obras completas*, IX, ii, 51.   [2] *Ibid.* 63.
[3] H. R. Romero Flores, *Reflexiones sobre el alma y el cuerpo de la España actual*, 32.

Figueras, the first president, disappeared—took the train for France—after a few weeks. His enemies—and most historians seem to have been his enemies—attributed his defection to cowardice; the real reason seems to have been the sudden death of his wife, which completely unnerved him. He was followed by Pi y Margall, whose authoritarian intransigence frightened the middle classes; while his federal system, applied without due preparation, had everywhere favoured the elements of disorder. Several provinces had proclaimed their autonomy, and rose against the central power of Madrid; the south was becoming full of independent, federal republics.

On the 18th July, 1873, Pi y Margall resigned, and by 119 votes to 93 Salmerón was elected to succeed him. Salmerón had also been a federalist, and was doubtless still federalist at heart. But confronted by a Carlist rebellion in the north, by the complete dislocation of the south through federalism pushed to extremes, and by threats of a Bourbon restoration in the near future, his first task was the re-establishment of law and order and respect for the central power. By the 4th August Seville had surrendered to General Pavía y Rodríguez de Albuquerque; Valencia was surrounded and ready to submit; Cartagena and Cadiz remained but could not last long. But Salmerón was a humanitarian. He was strongly opposed to the death penalty; and though he declared in the Cortes on the 8th August that he would allow neither the rebellion of the Carlists nor the insurrection of the Communes to go unpunished, yet he added that he would spare the lives of all citizens concerned in them. On the 4th September the Cortes rejected two amendments moved by him to a bill introducing, or legalizing, the death penalty in cases of national emergency or armed rebellion; and on the 7th Salmerón resigned.

Elected (he said) by a majority of the House as head of the government, he found that that majority, and with it the opinion of the country, imposed on him the necessity of establishing discipline in the army and putting an end to the civil war by recourse to methods which, if he considered them indispensable, were contrary to the dictates of his conscience. He did not feel himself with the strength to act contrary to the impulses of his own soul; and he regretted therefore that he could not continue to govern.[1]

"He left the throne to the executioner" (as Francisco Giner said afterwards),[2] and Castelar was elected to succeed him.

After the forcible dissolution of the Cortes by General Pavía (January, 1874) and the proclamation of Alfonso XII at Saguntum by General Martínez Campos, in the following December, Salmerón was deprived of his chair in the university and exiled to Lugo. He had naturally associated himself with Francisco Giner and those who had protested against the second decree of Orovio; and proceedings were to be taken "with no manner of delay or 'contemplation' against all who did not subordinate every criterion of scientific inquiry to the recognition of monarchist and Roman Catholic dogmas, and every principle of education to the 'indispensable' maintenance of the methods and discipline of scholasticism".[3]

The *alcalde* (mayor) of Lugo somewhat tactlessly invited the exile to take part in an official religious function, and received this crushing reply:

That is impossible. Assistance at an act of worship presupposes a feeling of pure devotion in the soul, without which one falls into profanation or hypocrisy. Out of respect to those very beliefs which I cannot share, I must abstain from attending any public manifestation of them. It would be illicit for me to do more than contemplate them from afar, in order to understand and estimate the amount of religiosity which they represent, and thus to affirm with reference to other communions with no religious spirit of their own, that which (thank God), to some pure spirits, and even to my own humble efforts, is no stranger to my conscience.[4]

The *alcalde* must have been puzzled by this rigmarole. Salmerón always wrote and spoke as if he were addressing a public meeting, and just then he was suffering from a feeling of

---

[1] Altamira, *Obras completas*, IX, ii, 63–4.

[2] F. Giner, *Homenaje a la buena memoria de don Nicolás Salmerón y Alonso*, xii.

[3] Aguilera y Arjona, *Salmerón*, 16.   [4] *Ibid.* 16–17.

justifiable annoyance. An era of reaction and dictatorship had set in; he himself was an exile, and it was clear to him that the real dictators were to be the bishops and the members of the religious orders. And what a dictatorship it seemed! The conservative party had always presented itself—almost as if it had held that office by title of hereditary nobility—as the sworn defender of those great social institutions, religion, property and the family. Yet the first act which that conservative party had accomplished was that of attacking the conscience of men, and precisely in that sphere and order of life in which conscience was most sacred, if indeed in spheres of conscience it were possible to establish hierarchies and consider one conscience more sacred than another. It had attacked those men who had made a profession of consecrating themselves to truth, exempt from all aim and interest of party, attentive only to the young whom the sacred ministry of teaching put into their hands. And this attack on conscience, if not for quantity, then for quality, had a representation and signification, which, saving the difference of time, might well place the name of Cánovas del Castillo, the reactionary premier, beside that of Torquemada.[1]

Salmerón was not an irreligious man, not "anti-God"—to use the elegant expression of modern propaganda. "Life without the religious spirit is a desert", he had written. For him, religion was what it was to some of his contemporaries in England: reverence, the love of an ethical ideal and the desire to realize it in this life. "The religious problem (Francisco Giner wrote) interested him for itself, and not only for its connexion with politics, although this aspect appeared to him to be the more important under the circumstances. The religious question awoke in his mind the deepest sympathy; but he resented persecution and the spectacle of whole classes deprived of spiritual intimacy, piety, humility, divine love and respect; cruelly dragged down, by terror and frivolity combined, to the outward servitude of liturgical materialism and the inward slavery of the 'compel them to come in'."[2]

[1] Salmerón, *En las Cortes de la Restauración, Homenaje,* 241.
[2] *Homenaje,* xix.

We must remember that both Salmerón and Giner de los Ríos lived in an age of bitter religious disappointment. Pio Nono's beginnings as a liberal Pope had ended in failure. "The old religion" had become a very new religion indeed, after the encyclical *Quanta cura* (1864), the *Syllabus* and the bull *Pastor aeternus*; many good catholics, in Spain as elsewhere, were driven out of the Church. Liberty of conscience, the independence of the civil power, popular sovereignty—all the foundations of the new social edifice, the ideals of all men of good will —were dismissed as "base follies, detestable and pernicious errors". Those pontifical pronouncements had come to seal the divorce of Roman Catholic dogma from modern civilization; while, as a result, thousands of voices of critics and reformers were declaring that the political and social emancipation of peoples depended on the denial of all religious principles.[1]

Salmerón left the country, and did not return until a general amnesty was proclaimed by the liberal government of 1881. Five years later he was elected as one of the members for Madrid, and the parties of the right found that they had caught a Tartar. Salmerón's ruminations in exile had embittered his irony and sharpened his tongue.

If it depended on him, he said (referring, in his first speech in a restoration Cortes, to the affront to parliamentary institutions offered by General Pavía),

If it depended on him, he would demand no other penalty than this: that the record of that deed of violence should be inscribed on the wall before them, adding beneath it the name of its author. With this, two things would be accomplished at the same time: firstly, a healthy admonition to all the elected representatives of the nation; and secondly, a means of providing the author of that deed with the immortality which, as it seemed, his fame as a soldier could not obtain for him.[2]

The restoration had been brought about by the most vulgar, base, opprobrious (they would say) of all actions, while

[1] Salmerón, *Crisis general en los pueblos cultos, Homenaje,* 127 note.
[2] *Homenaje,* 227.

they had merely wasted themselves in abuse and censure of those who had appealed to force. And that restoration, once brought about, was incarnate in one party, a party formed by means which they would call, with him, illegal. Further, the leader of that party (Cánovas del Castillo), who had promised so much, did not dare to re-establish civil marriage because the Nuncio of His Holiness would not give his permission. He had brought in no liberal reform, apart from public, oral justice as a timorous essay towards the institution of the jury system; nor had he done more than to restore timidly to their chairs those professors who had been deprived of them in the first days of the Restoration. In that way, he had left on the Statute Book all the measures which had been passed against revolutionary legislation, so that it was easy for a minister of the Crown (Pidal y Mon) to work surreptitiously under the inspiration of the school founded by St Ignatius to which the Right Honourable gentleman also belonged. (Laughter, and cries of Oh!) He would say that it was easy in the extreme for that minister to bring down all these reforms; and at that present time, if it had not been for the death of Alfonso XII, education would probably have become the exclusive patrimony of the religious orders. That was certainly a merit in the Right Honourable gentleman; that was, in a manner of speaking, an act of magnanimity in that spirit of almost Voltairean tolerance of the leader of the conservative party. But those were the facts revealed by the witness of reality.

(The Prime Minister: I thought the hon. member was a professor!)

The fact that he might be a professor, that in the name of liberty they were peopling the universities with men who represented the religious orders, that they granted them privileges which might not be enjoyed by societies of laymen, that there might spring from those conditions a spirit which would make it impossible to secularize education, what had all this to do with the fact that they still almost stood for toleration, and not for the principle which might support their own rights?[1]

[1] *Homenaje*, 235, 242.

Everything in Spain that was supported by the religious orders corresponded to a criterion which could no longer be said to be rooted in the public conscience, in any part of the world. A pure, noble and saintly ideal had become converted into miserable exploitation in which heaven was mortgaged for the enjoyment of earth. That was what the religious orders represented at that moment.[1]

Salmerón inveighing against the religious orders may move us to-day as little as Cicero inveighing against Catiline. Yet he is the authentic voice of the generation of 1868 on the eternal problem of Spain. Of greater importance is his statement of the legal position, in which he based himself securely on the work of Francisco Giner (in *La Persona Social*) and that school of jurists of whom the greatest English representative was Frederic William Maitland. He had always defended genuine associations, particularly of working men; his maiden speech had been a glowing defence of the International Union of Workers. But the religious orders (he submitted) could not be placed on the same level, *qua* Associations, with any other known corporate body. The Association, whatever the object of its existence, left the human personality of its members whole and intact. The existence of the Association was determined by the sovereign use of the will, which bound its members only in a particular and concrete relation; while the religious order bound by real bonds, bonds which were imperishable and indestructible over the whole human personality. In face of those conditions, could it be granted as a legal principle that man might make himself a slave? Was there not laid down in the bond of legality itself the great and perpetual power to re-make the will on new principles, according to the new demands of conscience? And if, by the side of this, they thought—though it was a purely secondary consideration—of what might happen in the economic order and in the implications of mortmain, how far had they to put back the clock in the course of history?

No (he went on), the religious orders did not possess the same binding force which other Associations possessed, in their legal

[1] *Homenaje*, 326.

origin, for other human objects. The religious orders, for the reason that they were determined in relation to an ideal beyond the grave, might be in flat contradiction with the demands of modern civilization; and for that reason there was incumbent upon the State the duty of supervision which it should not fail to exercise; for it was not convenient to hand over the charge of souls to those who might degrade or brutalize them. It was degrading to the soul at the present time to think that the monastic ideal might survive as a religion of human conscience. That ideal was a medieval ideal, the reason and legitimacy of which had disappeared; to-day the way to serve Society was by fighting with right for a weapon, spreading a moral sense among the masses, alleviating such misery and such suffering which existed, smoothing the differences between the man who possessed and did no work, and the man who worked and possessed nothing. And in that struggle, in the midst of which the Christian ideal was being worked out, here were those individuals with no need to do anything at all; solitary, lazy and inept, like all those who belonged to the so-called congregations.[1]

Then he turned to the question of education, of which, during the Restoration, the religious orders had succeeded in obtaining a large measure of control—not (he considered) in the best interests of teaching. Their instrument had been Queen María Cristina, second wife of Alfonso XII and mother of Alfonso XIII.

She proved (wrote A. E. Houghton, the historian of the Bourbon Restoration in Spain) that she not only relied on the support of the Vatican and the Prelates, but that she was determined to favour the Church and the religious foundations in every possible way. She became regent when Spain had felt the consequences of the expulsion of the Jesuits and other religious orders from France after the famous Jules Ferry laws, which aimed at placing these orders more under state control, to which they declined to submit. They selected Spain as an excellent field of enterprise; and it must be said that all the governments of the regency showed so much indulgence

[1] *Homenaje*, 326–8.

towards the Catholic revival thus started, that in less than a decade the kingdom was studded with more convents, monasteries, Jesuit colleges, catholic schools and foundations than had existed in the palmy days of the houses of Austria and Bourbon in the seventeenth and eighteenth centuries. A wave of clericalism and ultra catholic influence swept over the land, affecting the middle classes, the universities and learned societies, and making itself perceptible also among the governing classes and both dynastic parties, liberals and conservatives.

The right to be educated! (Salmerón cried in the Cortes). That was what constituted the sacred and inviolable liberty of conscience! For that reason, in modern times, the whole spirit of renovation and progress was opposed to giving instruction as a dogmatic imposition. That kind of instruction was a profanation of the conscience of the young, a violation of the pupil's most sacred rights; that his intelligence should not be educated except according to those laws and conditions which were determined by freedom of thought. Every situation, whatever it might be, in which the conscience was fettered, and the spirit atrophied by the relentless imposition of dogma, the will twisted by the hypocrisy to which proceedings more or less inquisitorial degraded noble minds, that situation would be radically, absolutely and definitely incompatible with the demands of modern education.[1]

He considered it an outrage, a violation of the child's conscience, to give him a sectarian education with the imposition of religious beliefs. The problem seemed at the moment to have been forgotten, but it would arise again;[2] and they might be sure that it would arise in such conditions that in the name of liberty people would be found to defend the privileges of the religious orders, in the name of liberty they would ask for teaching to be placed once more in their hands, to the exclusion of science and all kinds of modern knowledge.[3]

Further, there was a moral interest in emancipating education from the religious orders, and that was because the religious

[1] *Homenaje*, 330. [2] As it arose in 1933.
[3] *Pensamientos y fragmentos*, 38–9.

orders taught the young to lie. Among those orders was one which insinuated itself into the houses of the great, which even decided the direction of public business in a State like Spain, and which had invented the theory of mental reservation. What had it done for contemporary thought? He would give an example of what it had done. The Concordat stated that it was in the power of the government to establish three religious orders, and three only. What had been done was to create as many as were pleasing to Rome, or to each one of the Spanish bishops.[1]

They had to recognize the fact that Spain was a nation atrophied in the process of its development, and that that atrophy had been caused by a number of historical conditions, and above all by that which denied ethical virtue to every effort.and all energy directed to social questions, which was that which was rooted in the emancipation of conscience. A people which did not succeed in making itself free before the religious idea was a people condemned to base servitude, and to all the troubles of rebellion; and, oscillating between precisely those two terms, a servile people and a rebellious people, had been evolved a great part of the history of Spain, and particularly that of the nineteenth century.[2]

---

[1] *Homenaje*, 330–1. Under the Concordat of 1851 the law under which since 1836 the religious congregations had been banished from Spain had been so far relaxed as to permit the re-establishment of the Order of St Vincent de Paul, St Philip Neri and "one other among those approved by the Holy See".

In practice the phrase "one other" was interpreted by the bishops, not as one for the whole of Spain, but as one in each diocese; and at the request of the bishops congregations of all kinds established themselves in Spain, the number greatly increasing after the loss of the colonies and the measures of secularization in France, Portugal and Mexico.

The result was that "the regular clergy were fashionable and attracted the money of the pious rich, until their wealth stood in scandalous contrast with the poverty of the secular clergy. They also all of them claimed exemption from taxes; and, since many of them indulged in commercial and industrial pursuits, they competed unfairly with other traders and manufacturers". *Encyclopaedia Britannica* (11 ed.), xxv, 568–9, and *The Times*, 15 July, 1910.

[2] *Homenaje*, 496.

Salmerón's political activity was not limited to opposition in the Cortes. He could also be described as *político de acción*, a politician who could act when necessary. In office, he had been a good Minister of Justice; and a President whom everyone respected. In opposition, he organized, with Azcárate and others, the "Centralist" republican party. He worked hard and successfully for the pardon of General Villacampa, who (in 1886) attempted a republican *pronunciamiento*. Castelar had denied his support; Salmerón had been surprised by his precipitate action. But though they had not been taken into the general's confidence, neither Salmerón nor Azcárate was going to leave him in the lurch. Yet only after much work—and a piece of good fortune—was Villacampa reprieved...and transported for life. Salmerón also invented a solution for the "Catalan Question"—the so-called *Solidaridad catalana*; but it did not find the favour which it possibly deserved. The republicans of 1931 who brought in the Second Republic learnt much from Salmerón, and from the far-seeing definition with which, in his maiden speech, he defined the function of the party.

The republican party is not merely a political party, not merely a doctrinaire party, organ of the middle classes which may meet to discuss only the form of government, the organization of the powers of the State, and administrative action. It is a party which extends its patronage to a social tendency to serve the emancipation of the fourth estate, and prepare the free organism of equality, which must affirm for ever the rule of justice among men.

Salmerón was also a busy lawyer with a large practice. Though he regarded it less as a vocation than as a means of earning a living, he was inclined to treat it almost as a *sacerdocio*, a priesthood (as Azcárate said). It was said in the courts that his speeches were lectures on constitutional law; indeed the daily case of purely local interest, the civil conflict between two contending parties, he raised to the dignity of a universal problem of public and human interest.

One night, about 1897, two journalists went to see him after supper. He was just settling down to work at his briefs; but he got up and left everything to attend to his importunate visito rs. The time taken by them would probably have to be made up afterwards, and he would go on with his work until sunri se. "The expression on the face of his son showed a mixture of protest and resignation; but Salmerón seemed to enjoy being the victim of his friends and political supporters. His door was never shut to anyone; in that house they did not employ the subterfuge of saying that he was not at home. In vain the porcelain plate at the door advertised certain hours for con-sultation."[1] Salmerón did not run away or cut short an inter-view. He had not the technique of the great personage who can convey by a look or a gesture that the audience is at an end. He lived, perhaps, in less hurried times than ours; but his mind would be given up completely to his visitor, and he did not know, could not imagine, what it was to be in a hurry. He felt the intoxication of talk; and when his visitors did not arouse it, he provoked it himself and ran to meet it. Those who did not know him well imagined that it was only worth while hearing him speak in the Cortes, the lecture room or the law courts. That was not so. "Salmerón was eloquent, even in intimacy."

In the Cortes, members on the other side listened to him hypnotized, annihilated. They protested inwardly, but they were compelled to listen in silence. He could be severe, too, with his own party. "As a patriot first and a republican after-wards...", he said, in the course of a celebrated meeting held in a theatre. There was a storm of protest. Salmerón waited until it had blown over, and began the phrase again. There was another outburst; but Salmerón remained cool and collected, standing on the stage, and would not continue his speech until the phrase and the paragraph which followed had been correctly and completely delivered. Salmerón never left a phrase un-finished. In this he was helped by his training in philosophy and his constant exercise in logical thought. His oratory was part of himself, part of his fine figure and his ringing voice. Yet he was not a leader of men, not a founder of parties. He could

[1] *Pensamientos y fragmentos*, 16.

not work with men whose motives were less pure than his own. He was not really a parliamentarian; he was a prophet.[1]

Salmerón said, when he first entered public life, that he entered it only temporarily, and that his proper place was the university. His lectures, at any rate towards the end of his life, were generally at five in the afternoon. Groups of men, not all of whom had the air of students, might be seen waiting in the funereal corridors of the University of Madrid. Then there appeared

a tall man, like a St Paul,[2] with olive complexion and the face of a consumptive; large and expressive eyes, a moustache and a well-trimmed beard. He wore a frock coat which hung like a cassock, a soft biretta, stand-up collar and knotted tie; from the top pocket of his coat stuck out the corner of a white handkerchief.

He seemed a very polished democrat. He walked with his head down, but kept his penetrating gaze fixed. And as if to complete his person, he never went without his walking-stick, which he struck on the ground with fury and calm in turn. No one would have thought that this man could possibly be an ex-president of the Spanish Republic. As he passed the waiting groups, he greeted them with amiability and an exquisite courtesy.[3]

Salmerón's audience was characteristic. He generally had no official pupils; and when he had, they were few, and usually from the provinces. The horror which the University of Madrid felt for the lectures of Salmerón was surprising. "Do you know what you are doing?" a Madrid student asked one from Barcelona, who had just matriculated for the course. "You will only go there to masturbate your intelligence." In spite of that, Salmerón was never without a constant and regular audience composed of young and old, serious students, and amateurs not taking any special course of study. Saturday, the

[1] Information from a contemporary.

[2] It is recorded however that Paul was short (*Acts of Paul and Thecla*, 3) and the authority is said to be good.

[3] Carreras i Artau, *Introducció a la història del pensament filosòfic a Catalunya*, 255.

day devoted to ethics, came to be the great day of the week; and on that day among the increased audience Don Francisco Giner could be seen, listening attentively, "with the modest and simple manners of the eternal student"; while from time to time he took down a word or a phrase in a small note-book.

The author of this description, who was a pupil of Salmerón in his later years, goes on to describe him in the lecture room.

His first words, spoken in a low voice, with frequent pauses, were premonitions of a fair wind. Then the atmosphere gradually became more tense. We were in a full gale of rounded, sonorous periods.... Suddenly a thunderbolt, falling a few feet away, shook the attention of the audience: the Master, as if to underline an idea, had unexpectedly struck the table with his fist. Then Salmerón had reached the most interesting moment of his physical transformation. He had changed completely in face and figure; his look had an expression of plenitude, and his eyes, struggling to burst from their sockets, became terrifying. He seemed as if possessed. The tempest gradually subsided, but still rose now and again; until, from the back of the small lecture room a little door unexpectedly opened, and an intrusive voice exclaimed: "Señor Doctor, it's time!"[1]

What was he lecturing on? The philosophy of Kant; and all who ever heard him agree that he made an admirably lucid exponent. At times he would pause, and translate, directly from the German, passages from a book which he held in his hand: *The Critique of Pure Reason.*

"You must begin by freeing yourselves (he would say at the beginning of a course) from any sort of mental servitude. Lay aside all prejudice, acquired by the dogmatic imposition of someone whom you perhaps consider a master, or by the intromission of a minister of religion. We must work out our ideas without attending to any other demands than our own. In our inquiry into human knowledge, we must start from sensible experience which supplies us with data and phenomena; but it is necessary to recognize that the sub-phenomenal, the

[1] *Ibid.* 255-6.

thing in itself, always remains in a transcendent relationship; it is at the most a thought, never a thing seen."

His value lay in his power as an inspiring teacher, rather than an original philosopher, though he too had evolved in his own direction from the Krausist position of Sanz del Río. He rarely mentioned Krause, and indeed his most obvious link with that school of thought was Sanz del Río's pen, which was preserved in his study as if it were a holy relic. The ex-president of the first Spanish Republic had, indeed, undergone a notable evolution of thought. He could almost be classed with the neo-Kantians. The impulse given to Spanish philosophical thought by Krause and Sanz del Río had branched out in many different directions; and of these, the direction taken by Salmerón had been pursued farthest from the source.

The life of Salmerón is admired in Spain because it constitutes, above all, a model of the civic virtues; he will always be regarded as a mirror of conduct. The Spanish people is not likely to forget his renunciation of the presidency of the Republic of 1873, on a matter of principle, or his conscientious scruples for the revolution, which he aspired to make a national work, not the arbitrary imposition of a party. His detractors encouraged, with conscious injustice, the legend of his demoniacal pride. "It is not the *man* who is proud (said Valera, the novelist and diplomat), but the *idea*." There was indeed an "aquiline elevation" in his thought, served by a majestic delivery and a prodigious gift of the word: an "accent of Isaiah". Never (not even in Castelar) had Spanish political oratory so superb an incarnation.

His friends, in writing of him, unconsciously imitated his style.

Read the Catilinarian orations of Cicero, follow amid the great men of the French revolutionary assemblies the figure of Mirabeau; let your spirit thrill with the harmonious and many-coloured onomatopoeics of Castelar, adorn with all the enchantments of civic tradition the art of Demosthenes in his *De Corona*; you will not find an orator so majestic, of such insuperable grandeur or invective energy—the more tremendous the more he was opposed![1]

[1] Francisco Giner, quoted by Aguilera y Arjona, *Salmerón*, 11.

They brand him as an idealist, as unpractical (wrote González Serrano)—censures which are really eulogies—in every sphere in which his energies were applied.

The truth is that he passed beyond the general level of our public men (which is that of the common herd), and lowered that of many learned mediocrities and celebrities formed overnight.[1]

Among Spanish thinkers of to-day, he may be compared to both Unamuno and Ortega y Gasset. Unamuno is predominantly the prophet, Ortega the philosopher; but in Salmerón as in none other there was "the blend of prophet and philosopher, Semite and Greek, in his looks, his attitudes, his gestures and his words"; in none other, as in "that living statue which went about the world", could be seen "so happy a conjunction of the invincible athlete who during the combat could inspire with a look and whose ready heart with its youthful candour was always open to every kind of generosity and sacrifice".[2]

Seldom in modern times has a Spaniard received such eulogies, or deserved such eulogies; for they come from chosen spirits, unused to exaggeration.

He experienced everything: glory, prison, idolatry, poverty, exile; childish, open-hearted affection and venomous hate; the bitter magnificent heights of power and the austere joy of the sessions of silent thought. In almost the whole world of the spirit he had a hand, always after his own manner. And what a manner![3]

"As a man of action (Giner continues), Salmerón was disturbed by an unfortunate conflict. His general direction, in perpetual discord with his surroundings, the stern inflexibility of his character (which reminded one of Ríos Rosas), drove him out of parties and imposed upon him the solitary vocation of a prophet, called to stir the souls of his hearers with the might of his idea and the fervour of his passion."

His superiority, so disproportionate to the circumstances of his time, made him constantly a leader; but he was an eternal dissident,

---

[1] Aguilera y Arjona, *Salmerón*, 12–13. [2] León Vega, *Homenaje*, v.
[3] Francisco Giner, *Homenaje*, xix.

born neither to command nor to obey, one who bore along with him, without mercy, like a flood, the rebellious mass of his supporters, without the power or perhaps the will to be one with them.

"A leader must express the feeling of the group which he leads. He must be a conservative, a conformist, a personality at once elastic and firm, who leads the group to consciousness of itself, making it find in his words its unspoken aspirations, its inclinations and its repulsions."

"Salmerón was always struggling against his own leadership, against the tyranny of his destiny. For this reason, he was never freer than he was from 1868 to 1873, in that brief candle of the September revolution—so soon extinguished—in which, in despite of all convention and artifice, trusting to nothing but himself, he was at once a seer, a ferment, and a constant cause of disturbance, a soldier in all the causes which at the time of his death had been more or less won"—and now (it might be added) seem likely to be lost again.

IX

COSTA

the Voice

DURING the General Election of 1896, one of the candidates for a remote district in Upper Aragon visited his native place. He was not well known there; his chief work in the constituency—work which had made him famous all over Spain—had been performed farther up the valley, and in his birthplace he was merely remembered as one who had gone away as a child, had passed examinations, and become a lawyer in Madrid. Moreover, his own relations had a grudge against him, one that was quite sufficient to lose him their votes. Although a lawyer, he had refused to pervert the course of justice in the case of his step-sister's son, a poor half-wit who, through no criminal intent but from sheer stupidity, had been guilty of homicide, having knocked an old woman on the head when she accused him of driving cows through her pasture. The criminal had got safely over into France; but family pride expected that so eminent a lawyer would have done something to prevent the law from taking its course, should the half-witted nephew have seen fit to return to the scene of his exploit.

The eminent lawyer arrived one morning at his birthplace, supported by his sister's husband. He needed support in more senses than one. His great bearded head and gigantic body rested upon a pair of spindle legs and tiny feet. One arm was withered, and a form of creeping paralysis had already begun to overtake the lower limbs and trunk. The candidate's reception was chilly. Few of his political supporters were present, and they were unable to obtain a room in which to hold a meeting; the *caciques*,[1] the local bosses of the liberal and conservative parties, had combined to prevent them. They applied to the *alcalde*, for permission to speak in the public square. It

---

[1] *Cacique*, so called from the West Indian chiefs encountered by the conquistadores; *alcalde*, the "kaid", *i.e.* the mayor.

was refused; the *alcalde* was naturally the creature of one of the *caciques*. Seizing the arm of his companion, the candidate cried in a stentorian voice:

"To deal with this scum we want not words but weapons. Bring me a blunderbuss!"[1]

The great voice, as of one crying in a wilderness of hostility and misunderstanding, brought all the neighbours to their doors.

"Bring me a blunderbuss!"

The little group following him increased. A friend invited him to hold the meeting at an inn down by the bridge. The yard was not a large one, and the only possible platform was the window of a hay-loft—a window so small that it left no room for hands or body, and allowed the audience below to see nothing but the speaker's huge bearded face. The great voice began, but in a few moments the village band, sent by the *alcalde*, came down the street, passed by the inn, turned round and passed by again. There were protests and counter-cheers; boos, yells, hisses, and all the noises natural to a parliamentary election in Spain. The orator could easily dominate the voices, but not even he could be heard above the infernal din of the brass instruments; and, almost apoplectic from rage and shame, he withdrew his head into the hay-loft.[2]

Joaquín Costa shook the dust of Monzón from his feet once and for all.

The name of Costa was often on Don Francisco's lips. It has been impossible to keep it out of an account of the origins of modern Spain—as impossible as it was to suppress that great voice during the unadventurous period of the restoration—and this, even though Costa failed, and one of his biographers can describe him as "the great failure", *el gran fracasado*. Who was Costa?

Joaquín Costa, born in 1846, was a villager, the son of agricultural labourers. He was a clever boy but he had no money, and everything was against him. At the age of 17 he was minding the horse and cart which belonged to a small

---

[1] *Que me den un trabuco.*
[2] M. Ciges Aparicìo, *Joaquín Costa, el gran fracasado*, 13–15.

builder near Saragossa. His master gave him his dinner and lodging in a barn, but no wages; he had to find his own boots and clothes. When he went out with the cart, he was never without a song on his lips. Only two things disturbed him: the frisky horse, and his left arm which was already beginning to wither and was not strong enough to hold the animal in.[1]

He had forgotten almost everything he had learnt at the village school; but one October, he began to work for the *bachillerato* (school-certificate). His master stopped his dinner and only let him have his bed. In order to buy clothes and boots, books and food, he had to go to work, and found employment as a builder's labourer, while his school work was done by night. Reading opened to him a world of wonders which filled him with excitement; school-books were insufficient to satisfy his hunger for learning. He read everything he could get hold of, admired everything, wanted to know everything: science, art, history. He often sat up all night, reading and taking notes. In his first examinations he got three distinctions and two medals. He managed to be among the Spanish workmen sent to the Paris Exhibition of 1867, and then settled down at Madrid to study law. He had no money; he was always underfed and often on the brink of starvation. He persuaded the porter of a club (of which he was not a member) to lend him books out of the club library, without permission. He promised the porter a Christmas-box for his services: but when Christmas came round, he was unable to afford it. For a long time he possessed no socks and only one shirt, and in spite of his hard and unceasing work, he sometimes failed in his examinations and experienced more bitterly than most the consequent disappointment. He gave lessons in Spanish to a kind-hearted American, a Mr Tower, who paid him 2000 *reales* (about £20) and took him to Segovia and Ávila, La Granja and the Escorial.

At the proclamation of the republic in 1873 Costa was already a doctor of laws, and had great political ambitions. But he decided to stand apart from the struggle until his time should

[1] *Ibid.* 25.

come. "The proclamation of the Republic did not satisfy him. He foresaw its short life, and the restoration of the monarchy under Alfonso XII; in his own mind he gave this restoration ten or twelve years; his own opportunity would come afterwards, and he silently set to work to prepare himself for the task of governing." He had already thought out the main lines of his plan of reform; but he felt that he would have to be in power, like Cromwell, for at least a dozen years, to cure the ills from which Spain was suffering. As it happened, Costa was right in supposing that the reign of Alfonso XII would last for only ten or twelve years; what he forgot was that though kings die the monarchy continues, and it requires a great popular movement (like that which culminated on the 14th April, 1931) to change the form of government from monarchy to republic.

So with every possible disadvantage (balanced only by the fact that he was Aragonese, and gifted with a large measure of the stamina, obstinacy and downright mulishness of that remarkable race) Costa became in time a distinguished jurist— one of the few in Spain who really understood the "historicist" outlook of Savigny,[1] and the new views which had lately dawned in Germany. It is a tragedy that he never met Maitland; they would have found much to talk about, and many ideas in common. The charm and brilliance of that model Cambridge professor might have shown Costa that not all Englishmen were such as a disillusioned Spanish idealist, in his more bitter and anglophobe moments, might imagine them to be; and the Spanish jurist might have been described or even immortalized in one of those sparkling letters which Maitland could on occasion write to his friends. Alas, that he never got nearer Spain than the Canary Isles!

Costa became a learned authority on the customary law of Spain; he did valuable research on that subject as it concerned his native region of Aragon, in which he could speak of local usages and customs with first-hand knowledge. Yet under the Spanish system he could never be a professor, and his learned activity developed outside the official organization.

[1] Castillejo, *Minerva-Zeitschrift*, 204.

We have said that Costa had one advantage: that of being Aragonese. He was the last descendant of a long line of strong Aragonese characters, the reflexion of the hard, noble, fierce nature of the landscape and history of Aragon—distinguished for firmness, tenacity and constancy; by their rectitude, their love of independence, love of reality, of the soil, and of their own people.[1]

In his periods of hard work, his application terrified even those who were considered to be hard workers. He worked without ceasing for six days in the week, ate his meals hurriedly and went to work again. The seventh day was a day of rest for him, as for others; but he preferred to spend it in the country. In his own village, he liked to lie down under a tree; but when he grew older and his legs could only carry his great body with difficulty, he stayed in bed, and spent the day reading Jules Verne.[2] His nieces used to look after him, Balbina and Carmen:

"He got up about 11, and at once sat down to work. We brought up his breakfast between 12 and 1. When he felt stiff from sitting still, he would walk up and down for a few minutes—no more; for his lack of strength and his difficulty in walking did not allow him to remain standing for long. Now and then we could hear his voice— like a torrent it was—roaring out some song he had learnt in Andalucía when he was a young lawyer; you could hear it right down by the river. 'Are you happy, uncle?' my sister Carmen or I would say when he startled us with one of his songs. He would smile, and go back quietly to work. At nine o'clock at night, when half the people in the place were asleep—and all of them, if it was in winter— he asked for his dinner. He liked soup; and above all, *cocido*. He read while he ate it. About three in the morning, or four if he were in the middle of a piece of work, he called for his supper. We would be half asleep, and stiff with sitting up; but we wrapped ourselves up in blankets if it was cold, and my sister or I brought it up. My uncle never went to bed before four."

[1] Azorín, *Lecturas españolas* (Nelson ed.), 236.
[2] Altamira, *Obras completas*, IX, ii, 19–20.

"How many hours did Costa work?"

"From eleven in the morning until four the next morning—that makes seventeen hours."

Then Balbina added:

"As he got into bed, he took some sheets of paper, folded them so as to make about twenty little slips, and put them on the night table with a pencil beside him. When we came up at eleven to do the room, all the slips were covered with his tiny, clear writing."[1]

Costa is the symbol of the grief of Spain at the losses of 1898. He believed that all was over, and that his country could only hope to drag out its existence as a third class power. But earlier in life he had not been so pessimistic. Among his multifarious activities—and he read deeply and wrote with knowledge on every subject remotely connected with statesmanship and the good of his country—was a passion for geography, for colonization. "The first time", a friend wrote, "that I saw him, and heard him, was at the Geographical Society. He was holding forth on the exact position of Santa Cruz de Mar Pequeña. I was astonished at his eloquence; I marvelled at his knowledge. The whole history of Spain in its relations with Arabs and African Muslims came into his discourse, which was directed to showing how convenient it would be if Santa Cruz were a Spanish colony. He was at that time—1886, I think it was—an enthusiastic Africanist, a vehement patriot. All his knowledge, which was great, and his eloquence, which was extraordinary, were employed in spurring Spain on to the conquest and colonization of Africa, from Tetuan to the Atlas, and from Tangier to the Congo."[2]

Costa's love for geographical studies was older than that. It was aroused soon after his first arrival in Madrid. In 1872 he was already lamenting the fact of not being able to accompany De Lesseps on the adventure (which he too had thought of and begun to work out) of flooding the Sahara, and re-establishing

[1] Ciges Aparicio, *Joaquín Costa, el gran fracasado*, 24–5.
[2] R. Castrovido, ap. Ciges Aparicio, 94.

the great inland sea; and in 1875, when the same plan was being discussed in England and Italy, he wrote sadly

Poor Spain! Now Morocco can never be yours! Farewell, Spain across the Straits! Poor Costa! Now you will never be able to lead expeditions of discovery, and sail in a ship into the interior of Africa, so that it may be rapidly civilized. I was born too late; and *Spain has always been late everywhere, ever since it was struck by the paralysis of absolute monarchy.*

Costa might have written a much-needed history of Spanish unpunctuality; materials for such a history are to be found everywhere in his numerous published works, and it is tempting to trace the growth of procrastination as a method of life and government from the practice of Philip II—a sedentary, modern ruler in touch with the whole world from his study table, yet deprived of those modern means of rapid communication, which alone make the sedentary modern ruler effective. The Duke of Alba was not late in the Low Countries, nor was Spinola. What was late was the arrival of supplies and orders from home. No one realized this so well as Costa. From his earliest years he had been pessimistic as to the future of Spain. The disaster of 1898 helped to intensify that pessimism. Everything in Spain seemed to have come to a full stop, and the American victory affected the spiritual capacities of the Spanish people no less than the political future of the country. Costa seemed to see Spain "wandering unburied among the tombs of extinct nationalities".[1] Not only the State, the government, had failed, but the whole nation. "The fall", says Professor Altamira, "was considered to be so great as to show not only the consummation of the decadence which had already set in, in the second half of the seventeenth century—though certain reserves must be expressed on this last point—but even that it might be impossible for the Spanish people ever to rise again."[2] This national depression was shared even by opinion which was far from liberal: it was a state of mind which was general, and to

[1] García Mercadal, *Ideario de Costa*, 165.
[2] *Obras completas*, IX, i, 85.

be found amongst all Spanish people who were in any way concerned with the government of the country.

One result of this state of mind was the appearance of the
political and sociological literature known in Spain as "the
literature of 1898". The phrase has often been used in a slightly
different sense: for the poetry and prose of the writers who
afterwards came to be known as "The Generation of 1898".
But the writing which expressed the pessimism of the moment
and the acute dissatisfaction with the existing political order,
was, as a rule, the work of older men, and had little to do with
the generation of poets and novelists with whom contemporary
Spanish literature is justly held to begin, for they were very
young at the time and had hardly begun to be known. Some of
the younger writers certainly took an effective part in the
political events which were brought about by the American
victory; but, by their side, and with a much greater authority,
were others—rather older and rather better known—who took
a more important part: Macías Picavea and Joaquín Costa. Nor
should we omit the name of Ganivet, though his consular
appointments kept him far from the centres of Spanish life and
thought, and his importance has perhaps been exaggerated by
foreign students of modern Spanish history.

The political campaigns of that time were directed mainly
against the power of the *caciques* (who practically ruled the
country), and against the apathy and dishonesty in political
administration which that system fostered. These campaigns
(Professor Altamira points out) were not directed against this or
that form of government, but rather against the conduct of the
politicians, who, until then, had been at the head of affairs in
Spain. Among the writers and speakers who attacked these evils,
facile princeps was Costa. His pen and his voice were untiring. He
stumped the country, explaining to all who would hear him what
the political and economic situation really was. He demanded
an inquiry into the actual condition of the political system which
worked mysteriously in the shadow, and which had led to such
dire results in 1898; and he even suggested that various intel-
lectuals and university professors should be asked to conduct it.

Costa was a great maker of phrases. "We must put a double lock on the tomb of the Cid" was one of the most famous. By this he meant: "Our colonial dominion has ended. In the future we must give up all adventures of this kind; we must put an end to Spanish imperialism. We must only work for our own well-being in the country and for our own regeneration, if we wish to achieve anything useful and permanent".

From the sixteenth to the eighteenth century, Spain had been bled white. The drain of America had deprived it of the best and most generous elements of the race: the clearest and most impassioned intellects for truth and the cultivation of the spirit, the wills that were most steeled to resistance, the spirits that were boldest and most gifted with vital energy and initiative, the consciences that were most exemplary and of the highest moral temper.

The reverse of that process of selection, the drain of the monastic establishments at home and the intellectual dread of the Inquisition, combined with the colonization of Spanish America, had left Spain without a moral or intellectual *élite*: there were none to doubt and ask questions, none desirous of something beyond, none to plumb the depths of Nature and Spirit for their secrets....

It was calculated that the number of such persons removed by colonization and by monasticism reached half a million. Those who remained were of baser metal, the fools of every family; and that was the material which had been forming from century to century the population of modern Spain.[1]

At the same time he preached to all Spaniards something which he must have heard many times from Don Francisco Giner: that not everything should be expected from official support. Until then, it had been generally accepted that no social advance of any kind was possible without the support of the State. Nothing could be attempted without begging money from the government—money and moral support and at times even the framework of organization. Costa and the men of 1898 went on the opposite lines. "Distrust those principles! (they cried). That is not true! In every collective organization

[1] *Ideario*, 278–9.

which exists there are activities and energies which can very well be developed without the aid of the State. Some of the essential undertakings in modern life have not been carried out precisely because we waited for the men in high places to understand them and lend them their support. But they never did understand, and the most promising beginnings came to nothing. We must go to work in the opposite way—take the other road. We ourselves must work as hard as we can for our own social and economic regeneration, without taking the State into account at all."[1]

The Statesman should not occupy himself so much with making new laws, as with making men by means of education.... The art of governing a country consists principally in making oneself its tutor and taking it to school.[2]

The schools, of course, should be non-sectarian. As early as 1882 he wrote:

We must proceed to the total secularization of the existing schools; we must put an end to the eternal struggle with the politico-religious party, which stultifies all reform in education. The basis of concord must be the non-sectarian character of public instruction in all its grades.[3]

After schools, the next important thing was nutrition. The government should keep an eye on the cooking-pots of the people. It should aim, as its principal objective, at putting an end to this monstrous fact—a shameful testimony of backwardness—that, every night, more than half the Spanish people went to bed hungry.[4]

Costa was a great liberal. "He fought", as Altamira puts it, "for the expansion of every spontaneous activity in social life." He had been the defender of certain civil and local usages, *i.e.* the right to maintain any custom or piece of civil legislation which was peculiar to a definite region and reflected "the original juristic sensibility" of the inhabitants. As he came from Aragon, he had at the back of his mind a conviction of the

[1] Altamira, *Obras completas*, IX, i, 85. [2] *Ideario*, 256.
[3] *Ideario*, 113–14. [4] *Ideario*, 279.

exceptional importance of the civil institutions belonging to his own part of the country. But even so, he had been caught by the prevailing pessimism of 1898; and he had grave doubts whether at that moment it was possible to produce any collective movement in Spain, or whether such a movement would have the strength to carry out the transformation which, according to him, was necessary.

Spain (he said in 1899, just after the American defeat) did not need the blood of heroes and martyrs so much as *sang-froid*, brains, self-control, and good-will of all men. For more than a hundred years they had been in need of a *man*; but in those hundred years the reigning dynasty had not once been able to supply one, even as an exception. They wanted a man at the head of the State, not necessarily a superman or a hero or a genius—although that would be more effective and more likely to produce the desired result—but a man like some of those they knew, a Salmerón or a Giner. Spain had always been a majority of sane people governed by a minority of fools; the revolution he desired could not be brought about by the dynastic parties. It was at this moment that he began to consider, as a temporary expedient, the possibility of a dictatorship. It was not to be a military dictatorship, of course. Costa's dictatorship was to be a legal, juristic, "tutelary" dictatorship, *una dictadura tutelar*—a "surgeon of iron" who should operate quickly and save the country while there was yet time. He gave the exact meaning of his proposal when he submitted the subject to discussion at a debate at the Athenaeum. His exposition was preceded by a historical study of dictatorship in ancient Rome. That exposition had, as a matter of fact, been drawn up by a pupil of his, Don Rafael Altamira, afterwards to be the historian of Spanish civilization and a member of the Court of International Justice at the Hague. It showed that Costa's idea of a dictatorship had its foundations in the juristic conditions of Rome at a certain period, and that it was only a heroic remedy designed to accomplish reforms which, at that moment, could not be carried out (so Costa believed) by the spontaneous forces of the "colectividad" or by any other means. As soon as the activities of the "colectividad" arose again, the dictatorship was to end, and all would return to its normal condition. "I must add", Professor Altamira remarked—although he was writing under the dictatorship of Primo de Rivera, "that I did not entirely agree with my master's idea 'that this was the only remedy possible at the time'."[1]

Much has been said, both then and since, of the "iron surgeon", the *cirujano de hierro*, which Costa proposed. The most striking comments are those of Unamuno, who knew him well and in certain ways considerably resembles him.

The "iron surgeon", he remarks, "was only one of the many things in that imagination, that glowing rhetoric which used the phrase in the best sense, and behind which could be seen the work of a leader of men".[2] Costa's dictatorship never materialized; and the lamentable military dictatorship which existed from 1923 to 1930 was (as Unamuno characteristically expressed it) not made of iron, nor was it the work of a surgeon; it was rather the operation of a quack dentist. At that time there were some who exhumed things which Costa had said in order to justify the military dictatorship. "I believe that with Costa, as with a number of people who have a strong personality, one can dig up sayings to defend any point of view; for they are not people who move in a straight line, but live from a conjunction of inner contradictions, which is after all what gives life to most of us."

Costa was full of contradictions. His famous phrase has already been mentioned, "A double lock on the tomb of the Cid!" And yet, that man, who in this way expressed his passionate desire that Spain should abandon for ever all hope of another colonial empire and never more be led into colonial adventures, was (as we saw) often thinking how to keep the north of Africa for Spain. There was another contradiction, which Unamuno expresses with a characteristic paradox.[3] Costa

---

[1] Altamira, *Obras completas*, IX, i, 90.
[2] Speech delivered at the Ateneo de Madrid on the 21st anniversary of Costa's death.
[3] Unamuno, *Ensayos*, VII, 196 ff.

appeared as a republican: but his political programme, if it resembled any other political programme at all, was nearest to that of the Carlists.

Setting aside all questions of clericalism and absolutism, Carlism is the representative, with all the good points as well as the bad, of the old native Spanish (*castizo*) rural democracy—"monkish democracy", as Menéndez y Pelayo called it. Carlism may be said to have come into existence as a protest against the dissolution of the monasteries—the dissolution, not only of the property of the clergy and the religious orders, but of communal property as well.[1]

The "agrarian collectivism" preached by Costa, and his desire to return to that state of communal ownership, his "politics of shorts and sandals" (*de alpargata y calzón corto*)— all that (Unamuno considers) was sheer Carlism, though it was a Carlism without Church or King. Not that Costa did not believe in them. "I think that he believed in a king, although from historical conviction he execrated the Houses of Austria and Bourbon; that he believed in God, there is some doubt. He never spoke of it; he passed over it, put it on one side." "I have a certain suspicion" (Unamuno adds) "that perhaps he was not altogether convinced about the God of Aristotle, but I also suspect that he believed in the Virgin of the Pillar".[2]

Costa's mental reserves in matters of religion were perhaps not as great as Unamuno believes. They were probably dictated by prudence, and the desire of not involving his friends and supporters in the dangerous consequences of a quarrel with the Church. When, in later life, friends gathered round him at the Republican Club, he preferred to talk of history, art or agriculture rather than the iniquities of clericalism.

"Clericalism! Tell us something about that, Don Joaquín", a young anti-clerical remarked one day.

Costa made a gesture of annoyance. Then he winked.

"All we Spaniards have the blood of friars in our veins! Nobody should speak disrespectfully of his own father."[3]

[1] *Ibid.* VII, 211.
[2] On the 21st anniversary of the death of Costa.
[3] Ciges Aparicio, *Joaquín Costa, el gran fracasado*, 60.

Yet the man who said that could write:

The only legislator who has discovered the secret of true government is Christ...because he dealt not only with the understanding
but also with the will.[1]

Besides being a man of contradictions, Costa was a man of
solitude. In the Spain of 1898, research had to be carried out
by solitary workers, with no atmosphere or materials or en-
couragement for investigation; they had to do everything for
themselves. "A Spaniard who made a discovery in arts, science
or literature, signifies much more than those who have done the
same in other countries. For there, the researcher does not make
the discovery for himself; some of his companions in the work
really make it for him."[2]

Costa spent much time in working at things which had
already been done before. He always insisted, and rightly, on
going back to the original sources—a rare attitude in the Spain
of his time. When he was inquiring into certain things connected
with the decline and fall of the Roman Empire, he disregarded
everything that had been done on the subject, and went back to
the Roman writers themselves. "He shut himself up to re-
create a technical culture which in his time did not exist in
Spain." Costa (Unamuno remarks) always lived in history,
inside history, and for history alone. "All his ideas were
historical ideas; there was nothing in him that could be called
metaphysical. I should say that, rather than a Platonic spirit,
he was a Thucydidean spirit...for Plato is all very well, but
Thucydides is better."

As he took an historical point of view, so also he took a
traditionalist point of view—that of a man who lived by and for
tradition; and he was also in this sense a "traditionalist", a
conservative in the specific sense which the word traditionalist
has in Spain.

He was naturally and before everything a Spaniard. There was
no doubt about Spain hurting him! He encouraged the ideas of
europeización; he invented *europeización* in a fit of pure Spanishness,
because (like Job) he was a man of inner contradictions. He was a

---

[1] *Ideario*, 256.   [2] Unamuno, *loc. cit.*

man who lived by struggling within himself; and when he talked of the "Europeanization" of Spain, perhaps he meant also the "hispanization" of Europe. A Spaniard does not want to make Spain European, unless he is also trying to a certain extent to make Europe Spanish; that is to say, to take our things to them in mutual exchange.

He had an intimate feeling for tradition, and went to look for it in the most remote quarters: in the civilization and primitive culture of the Iberians. At a recent meeting of the Academy of History in Madrid (May, 1933), a member presented a summary of the present state of knowledge of the question of Tartessos, with special reference to the work of Professor Schulten. He quoted Greek and Latin texts to show the accuracy and importance of a book published by Costa in 1891 (*Estudios ibéricos*), a work which he described as one of the greatest efforts of Spanish erudition, and lamented the fact that, in spite of the undoubted merits of the book, it was never quoted by either Spanish or foreign authors, even though its conclusions coincided with those of Professor Schulten.[1] The nature of his work was hardly likely to attract the public in Spain, and it was not of such a character as to attract attention abroad, like that of Cajal (pp. 82–3). Unamuno has explained why that was. "Costa's investigations in the Spanish manner could not give him, outside Spain, the credit which Cajal achieved with research conducted on recognized European methods. Costa lived and laboured in comparative isolation; and a certain restlessness and a curiosity for all sorts of things drove him to write upon every possible subject, and to scatter his intellectual activity in various fields.... He never became a specialist."[2]

Yet though solitary, he did not always work alone. When he was studying the ancient customary law of the different regions of Spain, different people brought contributions to his work—Unamuno, for instance, brought an account of the ancient Fishermen's Guilds in the Basque Provinces—for this solitary and disappointed man (like the more sociable and more hopeful Don Francisco Giner) had the virtue of setting others in

[1] *El Sol*, 17 May, 1933.   [2] *Ensayos*, VII, 196.

motion and encouraging them to work, of being a centre, a focus, for a large number of other workers. That was how he wrote his studies in Agrarian Collectivism in Spain, seeking out the old traditions of a profoundly democratic organization among the villages, a tradition which had gradually become obscured or died out.

Spain grieved him profoundly, hurt him. He would sometimes break out into wild imprecations against a people which he saw to be sunk in irreparable apathy. How many times did he not tell them to their faces—the whole Spanish people—that they were "eunuchs"?

"And you should have seen him weep with rage," Unamuno adds, "especially towards the end of his life. I remember once when he came to a festival at Salamanca, he said:

"'Next year, perhaps, we shan't be able to do this. We shall all be subjects of the United States'.

"His voice broke, and a sigh cut thro' what he was saying."

That man was a man who lived on his passions, and on the contradictions in his own soul; on grief at the thought that he was dying without realizing the dream of his life: the Spain of a thousand-year-old tradition, in which were all the possibilities of a thousand-year-long future.

Joaquín Costa and Francisco Giner represent two ways of regarding history, two attitudes towards politics. Don Fernando de los Ríos relates that one day in the Spanish Record Office—the Archivo Histórico Nacional—Costa found an early Spanish poem beginning:

Castille seemed a province that had been laid waste; and its towns, fields without cultivation; the soldiery naked, the nobility barefoot, the people beggars: all action cramped.

He showed it to Don Francisco.

"Giner," he said, "that is Spain."

"No, Joaquín", Giner answered. "That *was* Spain. Spain is different now."

"Giner, we want a man."

"Joaquín, what we want is a people."

X

AZCÁRATE
the Chairman

LEÓN is a Roman town in the north of Spain. Its name is, literally, "Legion", for the Seventh Legion made its permanent camp there in the first century B.C., and it still retains considerable Roman walls and towers. A thousand years later it was the capital of a kingdom, León, while Castille was still a county; the burial-place of its kings is second to none in the strange solemnity of the round, Romanesque arches, and the soaring beauty of its Gothic cathedral is surpassed nowhere in Spain. A ballad relates that the Count of Castille, summoned to Parliament in León by King Sancho the Fat, rode into the town on so fine a horse and with so perfect a hawk on his wrist, that the King insisted on buying them, promising that if the money were not paid by a certain day, the amount due should be doubled for each day's delay. Seven years went by, and the Count of Castille no longer obeyed the royal summons to Parliament. The money had not been paid, he said, and it amounted to a very large sum, so large indeed that in the end the price of procrastination could only be paid by the independence of the county. Castille became a separate kingdom, and León learnt a lesson which its strong-minded, punctual inhabitants have never forgotten.

In León, they say, the only illiterates are the strangers. That will be true some day, for the Leonese have a passion for building schools and endowing them so as to make them independent both of the State and the Church. There was, for instance, Don Francisco Fernández Blanco de Sierra Pambley, a cattle-dealer on a large scale, one of whose forbears had been Finance Minister in the time of Ferdinand VII. Though an ardent liberal, and latterly a republican, he had a great respect for everything old, and he always said that he had two ambitions: to preserve his inheritance undiminished and devote the income to the foundation and support of schools, of which he built and endowed no less than fifty-four.[1] He lived part of the year at Villablino (a small mining town in a remote and mountainous part of the province), in a severe nineteenth-century house where, in 1886, he founded a mercantile and agricultural school. Then he turned his attention to the village of Hospital de Orbigo (where Suero de Quiñones once "kept the bridge", like a second Horatius, in the *paso honroso*, and where, it might be added, there is a stream with the trout "shouldering each other out of the water"), and there he founded a continuation school, an agricultural school and a school for girls. At Villameca and Moreruela de Tábara (where he sheared his sheep) he established two continuation schools to supply the deficiencies in the primary education given by the government and the religious orders. In León itself he built an industrial school for work-people, a school of agriculture, a school for girls, and a school for some thirty boys whose fathers were usually railwaymen and who were required to know their "first letters" before being admitted. All of these institutions (which cost him nearly £200,000) Sierra Pambley built, endowed and directed himself, with a board of advisers including Francisco Giner, Cossío and Azcárate. If his house in Villablino was new, that in León was old—a mansion opposite the cathedral, in the corner of the square, with great doors studded with iron nails and a knocker which seemed as if it would wake the dead when his guests from Madrid used to arrive (as the train from Madrid used to arrive) between two and three in the morning.

Sierra Pambley's rugged personality was reflected in his regular habits. He spent the winter in Madrid, where he was constantly in touch with Francisco Giner and the "Free Institution". The first week in May was sheep-shearing; and he was off to the pastures at Moreruela de Tábara. Then he would ride on, through Benavente, to Hospital de Orbigo, where he awaited the passage of his flocks on their way up from winter pastures in the south. Until July, he remained in León; and then

[1] A. and A. García Carraffa, *Azcárate*, 272–3.

spent the rest of the summer at Villablino. Then he retraced his steps, following the return of his flocks to the south; and on the 1st November, Giner, Cossío and Azcárate could count on him in Madrid. Until well over 80, he made most of his journeys by mule, dressed in the style of the country. Once having become republican he never wavered; and he settled his religious doubts by never attending church in Villablino, but by generally going to service at Moreruela. He looked after his institutions himself. He lived near them, and liked to be able to see them when he looked out of the window. He had no children of his own, and for that reason directed all his paternal sentiments to the protection of children and their education and to giving them a start in life.

His example bore fruit. The Leonese were not going to let Sierra Pambley do everything. In strange contradiction to the rest of Spain, where everyone waits for government to take the first step, and expects everything to be done from above, individuals in León began to follow his example and do things for themselves. One village (Sosas de Laceana) built its own school, with no contribution from the village council and still less from the State. In León itself, Julio del Campo, a quarryman who had made money, built a school in memory of his father-in-law, adorned it with busts carved by his own hand and his nephew's, and inscribed thereon the letters of the alphabet, the numerals and the names of his companions, the quarrymen, stonemasons, carpenters, and smiths who had helped him.

Into this atmosphere of pride, independence and endeavour was born, on 13th April, 1840, Gumersindo de Azcárate. His birthday was the day of the extravagant Visigothic Saint, San Gumersindo, whose name he accordingly bore; but he sometimes confided to friends that he wished his name had been simpler.

The Azcárates were north-country people "on all four sides", as they say in Spain. His paternal grandfather, Tomás de Azcárate, came from Navarre, and the name certainly sounds as if it were of Basque origin. He married Clara del Corral, a lady from Bedoya, near Santander. His grandfather on the other side was Luis Menéndez Morán, a colonel of artillery who was born in Gijón, the principal sea-port of Asturias, and married a lady from the same town, María del Carmen Nava. Patricio de Azcárate (the father of Gumersindo) was born in Gijón about 1800, and went to college (from 1820 to 1823) at the Institute named after that enlightened anglophile of the eighteenth century, Jovellanos. Even as a boy Patricio began to resent the reaction and repression of Ferdinand VII; his behaviour as a student, the speeches that he made and the articles that he wrote, brought down on him a strange and terrible ecclesiastical penalty: that of *impurificación*. His father was naturally somewhat alarmed; the Inquisition had been re-established, its prisons were still in working order, and the "Secular Arm" might even be invoked as it had been in the past. Patricio de Azcárate bethought him of Santiago de Compostela where he had a friend who was a canon of the cathedral; he lost no time in making the journey and explaining to the good canon what had happened.

Under the ban of *impurificación*! Holy heavens! How could an old friend like Don Tomás have a son who was such a *liberalote*! In the end, he became quite attached to the boy; but the ecclesiastical *impurificación* stuck; and later, when Patricio gained the title of "advocate" in the chancery at Valladolid, it was expressly stated that, on account of the *impurificación* of 1823, he had no jurisdiction. That, however, did not prevent him from being appointed Civil Governor in various provinces, Biscay, León, Toledo and Murcia, and he occupied his leisure in reading philosophy and cultivating the acquaintance of men such as Sanz del Río and Fernando de Castro, with whom the reader of this book will also have become acquainted in an earlier chapter. Patricio de Azcárate married a lady from Gijón, Justa Menéndez Morán y Nava, who was destined to be the perfect mother of a large family. Two boys died in infancy; then came Gumersindo and two brothers, Tomás and Cayo, one of whom became an admiral and the other a colonel of engineers. There were four daughters, of whom Manuela, early left a widow, came to keep house for her eldest brother in Madrid.

The family lived in a fine old house in León, in the Calle de la Rua. It had a curious history, for it had once been a synagogue, which had been abandoned on the expulsion of the Jews in 1492; and that was sometimes given as the reason why Gumersindo had turned out "rather a Rabbi". His first schoolmaster bore the curious name of Cid—Don Angel Cid; then, at the age of nine, he was sent to learn Latin with a dominie called Don Justo, who went on the principle that blows were the best stimulus to the intelligence. At ten, he entered the Instituto, and showed a remarkable aptitude for mathematics—and for asking questions. He was lively, cheerful, communicative and rebellious; "Notes excellent; behaviour reprehensible" was his usual report. One day, during a lesson on religion and morals, the master spent the whole hour defending the Inquisition. Gumersindo listened attentively, and then suddenly said: "But sir, if the Christians were right to burn heretics, then the Pagans were right to martyrize believers." The next stage was the University of Oviedo, where he matriculated in 1855, taking law in deference to his father's wishes and science in accordance with his own. Science, however, was becoming a dangerous subject; in 1857 it was suppressed and might no longer be taught or studied in the university. Gumersindo turned to politics; at debates in the Ateneo he defended democratic ideals: liberty of conscience, liberty of worship and civil marriage—ideals which in most countries have long become commonplaces, but which, in Spain, are still bitterly attacked in the pulpit and used as weapons against the "godless" Second Republic.

From 1858 to 1861 Azcárate was at the University of Madrid. He took the degree of licentiate in laws, and learnt to speak in public in a "discussion circle" which met at the house of the Marqués de Heredia. He was appointed to a government office (*Dirección General de los Registros*) which was afterwards incorporated in the Ministry of "Grace and Justice". More important still, he was received by his father's friends Sanz del Río and Fernando de Castro, and at once found himself in the innermost circle of the philosophic radicals who were

to be the spiritual and intellectual leaders of the generation of
1868.

In the nineteenth century there were certain English and
Scottish families, settled in Spain, which had an extraordinary
influence over all Spanish people with whom they came in
contact. They are, indeed, no less ancestors of the generation of
1868 than the German philosophers of the school of Krause, or
George Borrow and his fellow-travellers for the Bible Society.
Neither Krause nor Borrow would, perhaps, have recognized
their ideas as they grew up on Spanish soil, though they would
have admired the integrity of character and ethical sensibility
which those ideas produced. The families of English and
Scottish business-men and consuls, when once they had gained
the confidence of their Spanish acquaintances, found that there
were some Spanish people very different from what they had
imagined, men possessed of moral qualities which they admired
and social gifts which they appreciated. The English, and even
the Scots, found that they might have something to learn from
their Spanish visitors; while the Spanish visitors found themselves face to face with something at that time unknown in
Spain—a Victorian drawing-room. This is said in all seriousness.
It was the Victorian drawing-room, and the standard of behaviour which that institution required and produced, which
gave Spanish people their ideal of "the poetry and refinement
of English customs". There were also Spanish men who had
married English wives, and through whom the Victorian
drawing-room might be said to have been imported. Pascual
de Gayangos married a Miss Fanny Revell, of Round Oak,
Windsor; and their daughter, Emilia (who was educated in
England and married the cultivated anglophile, Juan Facundo
Riaño), had a drawing-room in which Victorian austerity and
antimacassars were relieved by Hispano-Mauresque pottery,
ivories, pictures, and all the lovely medieval Spanish things
which a cultivated collector in the nineteenth century was in
a position to acquire. Sigismundo Moret, the distinguished
liberal statesman, ambassador in London for King Amadeo, a
friend of Francisco Giner and Azcárate and one of the founders

of the Free Institution, also had an English mother, Aurora Prendergast, who, though born in Madrid, was the daughter of an English general and brought up *a la inglesa*, "her spirit saturated by surroundings of fineness and elegance, her figure one of the most exquisite, attractive and distinguished which adorned court festivals in the time of Isabella II".[1]

The representatives of Victorian England who made friends with Azcárate belonged to the family of Innerarity. They were doubtless of Scottish origin; the name—in what is probably its original form, Inverarity—is known to-day in Glasgow, Montrose and North Berwick. The head of the family in question had been born in Florida when it was still a Spanish possession; and he had relations in Cuba. Emilia ("Emmy") had been sent to school in London, and at nineteen so wound herself about the affections of Azcárate that they were married after a comparatively short engagement. Both would probably have preferred a civil marriage, but in Spain at that time there was no such thing. Emilia seems to have been a Roman Catholic; but Azcárate, though he was then and always remained a good Christian, could not honestly say that he was also a good Catholic, and the witty Irish subterfuge of calling oneself a "bad" Catholic would not have appealed to him. Licence to perform a "mixed" marriage (*i.e.* a marriage between a Catholic and a non-Catholic) was sought and refused, and the marriage was celebrated canonically, on the 5th October, 1866. Their happiness was shortlived. Emilia died within a few months (29th April, 1867), giving birth prematurely to a son, who died within 30 hours. Azcárate went to live with the Inneraritys, and remained with them until 1873 when they built a villa at Hendaye, just over the French frontier, and then he frequently spent the summer with them. They must have helped him with his work, especially in the matter of English translations, such as Mackenzie's *Roman Law* "translated by Gumersindo de Azcárate, and compared with the Spanish in collaboration with D. Santiago Innarity (*sic*)", and Fawcett's *Free Trade and Protection* "translated from the English in col-

[1] A. de Olmet y A. García Carraffa, *Moret*, 23.

laboration with D. Vicente Innerarity". The family has since been naturalized Spanish.

In 1884 Azcárate married again. The lady was Doña María Benita Álvarez Guijarro, daughter of a former Minister of Grace and Justice and president of the Cortes before the revolution of 1868. In the Constituent Cortes of that year he was the only member (it is said) who favoured the candidature of Alfonso XII; but, by command of Isabella II, he never took his seat. Once again permission was sought for a mixed marriage. The bishop of Madrid, "who confessed to a real friendship for Azcárate", worked hard to obtain a licence. The pontifical document, when at last it arrived, contained the condition that the marriage should not be celebrated on Spanish soil, and the ceremony was performed at Lisbon, with the blessing of the Cardinal Patriarch and in the presence of the Spanish minister, who happened to be Don Juan Valera, the well-known man of letters. This was said to have been the first "mixed" marriage ever celebrated between Spanish subjects. Doña María Benita died childless in 1902.

The revolution of 1868 caught Azcárate when he was twenty-eight, while he was still young enough for enthusiasm and old enough to realize how the opportunity was lost. The "September Revolution" is a dividing line in modern Spanish history. No one who was not living at the time (as Moret said long afterwards) can realize how different those days before 1868 were from anything we know now; for the so-called "Restoration" of 1876 restored nothing but the dynasty, while in religion, politics and education it brought a new and considerably more rigid world. Azcárate and Giner preserved the open, inquiring minds of 1868 along with a sense of seriousness and responsibility in an age which had little sense of either. Life, in their view, was not necessarily tragic, but it was serious; their ideals, and the Institution which expressed them, were the Noah's Ark—to use the expression of Ortega y Gasset— tossed on a flood of dishonesty, jobbery and pretentiousness, in which Spanish culture was saved from destruction during the great flood of reaction after 1876.

Azcárate was first appointed lecturer in Political Economy at the University of Madrid, and then, in 1873, professor of Comparative Legislation, which was, in a sense, his life's work. He was asked to stand as a parliamentary candidate for León. He was defeated. He was known as a supporter of Salmerón, whose moral authority over the republican party he shared; and he was invited by a namesake, Nicolás Azcárate (a Cuban, and no relation of Gumersindo) to join the staff of a new daily paper, *La Voz del Siglo*, "The Voice of the Century". For a time he wrote a daily leading article, basing his position on four points: (1) the legality of political parties, (2) free trade, (3) freedom of the colonies, and (4) civil marriage. The editor-in-chief was Moret, who was afterwards to be Colonial Minister at the time of the Spanish-American war; and they both defended a measure of reform which ought to have been granted then, and might perhaps have avoided the loss of the remaining Spanish colonies to the United States—Home Rule for Cuba. When the monarchy was restored with Amadeo of Savoy, Moret went as ambassador to London; and Azcárate, though a stout republican, was ready to support any king "deserving of sympathy and the support of the people". He used to relate a curious episode which happened at that time.

I was a civil servant, and had to go to the Palace on the King's Saint's-day, to a levée. On entering the throne-room, my attention was distracted by all that queer collection of uniforms. I looked at the group formed by the Diplomatic Corps, the Government, the Grandees...and was so absorbed in contemplation, that I filed by with my colleagues, without having seen the King.

When we had left the throne-room, I said to Moscoso, who was beside me:

"And the King? Where was the King?"

"Didn't you see him?" (he answered) "Why, on the throne, of course".

I hadn't noticed any such thing, and regretted my distraction, thinking that the monarch must have taken it as an act of discourtesy that I had not bowed to him, like the rest of my colleagues.[1]

[1] A. y A. García Carraffa, *Azcárate*, 50.

During the republic of 1873 Azcárate went quietly on with his lectures at the university. Salmerón insisted that he should become head of his department at the ministry, but he agreed with reluctance and refused to accept the increase in pay. The restoration brought with it the dismissal of the professors, already described in the case of Don Francisco Giner. Azcárate, exiled to Cáceres in Estremadura, employed his leisure in writing. He wrote a good deal, for his exile lasted for five years; but after it was over and he had entered fully into politics (he was member for León from 1886 until shortly before his death), he had neither the time nor the inclination to concentrate on literary work.

One of the first things which Azcárate wrote (or finished) in exile was the *Minute of a Testament*,[1] a strange "ingenuous and romantic work", but one of considerable psychological interest. Nothing can be imagined more like the man, or his epoch. A reader of to-day feels as if he were visiting an old house in a Spanish provincial town, the rooms full of glazed cabinets and whatnots, a model of the fountain in the Court of Lions under a glass shade and a map of London at the time of the Great Exhibition of 1851. Azcárate's *Minute of a Testament* is the history of a nineteenth-century soul and its religious difficulties, cast in the form of notes for a will. In length it is little more than a pamphlet; the voluminous notes were added (Azcárate said afterwards) in the proofs, so that the work might reach the number of pages necessary to make it pass legally for a book, and thus escape the censorship to which the government of the restoration subjected any publication in pamphlet form.

"W" begins with old-fashioned portraits, of his father and mother, faded as daguerreotypes yet firm enough in outline to show that, though the background is slightly altered and the velvet curtains looped about the massy pillar in a slightly different way, the portraits are Don Patricio and Doña Justa, the father and mother of Azcárate himself.

[1] *Minuta de un testamento, publicada y anotada por W...*Madrid, Suárez, 1876.

My father, born of the middle class, was a doctor by profession; and perhaps for that reason a supporter of the scientific and religious movement which began in our country with the present century. Under the inspiration of French philosophy and of the revolution of 1789, he had abandoned in his inner consciousness the religious beliefs of his fathers and embraced with secret enthusiasm the new political doctrines, serving the former in a disinterested and patriotic manner and submitting himself in respect of the latter to the almost obligatory hypocrisy which to a certain extent the times imposed. (Note. This frankness in political opinions and dissimulation in religious beliefs is a contrast which, unfortunately, has existed in our country without interruption up to the present day....)

Fortunately, through lack of this eternal basis of morality, I was greatly helped by the respect he paid to every lofty principle and every great idea; for the maxims which I heard from his lips and witnessed in his acts were for me like the sacred canons of the moral law—a morality rather of sentiment than of reason, it is true, but appearing to my spirit as infallible as the security of the bond which united me with him to whom I owed my existence.[1]

Then Azcárate gives a portrait of his mother, so exquisite that we can almost hear the sound of her voice and catch a fleeting glimpse of the tilt of her chin.

My dear mother belonged to a distinguished family, and preserved those good qualities which are still to be met with in our gentry, combined with certain prejudices from which it has not yet been able to free itself. Complying scrupulously with the practices and duties of her religion (though she never fell into the extravagances of mysticism), firm in her faith and the love of her husband, more than once she must have been beset by doubts and have felt torn within herself at observing, drawn up against one another, the representatives of the Church and the party in which the companion of her life had elected to serve.

As a true Christian she was inspired by charity, and from duty and affection felt herself attracted to the weak and unfortunate. But certain prejudices of her class prevented her from harmonizing the

[1] *Minuta*, 4–5.

equality of the Gospel with the inequality of the social conditions
presented by everyday life.

"W" admits the same prejudice in himself.

For this reason, I, who from the time I was a boy have been inclined to look upon all men as equal, have had to wrestle with a
certain repugnance which acting in conformity with this principle
produced in me; and it was somewhat late in the day when I came to
understand that justice and respect, help and consideration are owing
to all, but that friendship, confidence and intimacy are only due to
those who deserve them.

Under the care of his mother "W" received his first lessons,
and his religious instruction. His moral training was due to
example. Every act which he witnessed in the bosom of his
family was engraved on his mind more deeply than anything
he learnt in the Catechism; the judgments formulated in his
hearing by his father and mother were sentences from which
there was no appeal.

Then he describes his education in "the so-called humanities";
the only useful thing he learnt (he says) was to translate easily
from Latin. He studied medicine, without particularly caring
for it:

I had no great desire to practise; I had no vocation to do so, nor
(after thinking the matter over conscientiously) did I feel that I
should ever have enough knowledge for the purpose. On the other
hand the world of science, which was what attracted me, seemed
closed to me on all sides; and at the same time I considered it a
point of honour to earn my own living and not be a burden to my
parents now that I was twenty-five years old and had a profession of
my own.[1]

In the end, "W" became a lecturer in physiology; and the
study of natural science as apart from medicine was not without its effect on his religious beliefs. The crisis began by his
doubting the literal truth of the biblical cosmogony; "and
since catholicism is a system in which everything is related and

[1] *Minuta*, 15.

everything will fall to the ground when there is no longer belief in the divine inspiration of the sacred books, the first doubt which assailed my spirit produced in me a general uncertainty because I saw at once that it affected that which was most important to man in his whole life". A more recent solution, according to which the important thing is not the truth of revelation but the fact that for centuries a large number of people have believed it to be true, would not have occurred to Azcárate. He would have thought it too dishonest for serious consideration.

While he clung desperately to the faith which he felt to be gradually but inevitably slipping away from him, he was faced by two problems, "between which there could not fail to be a certain relation", problems which commonly arise at the age of puberty: faith and marriage.

During the years of our amorous relations (he says, describing his courtship) in proportion as our intimacy ripened, confidence increased, and at last there were no secrets between us, nor any thing or any idea belonging to the one which was not taken as belonging to the other: chances of life, hopes, dreams, fears, all these we told one another...except those which were concerned with our religious beliefs....

In the midst of my doubts, I believed in God, in religion and in Christ; and holding it to be a grave matter to abandon my faith without previous and mature consideration, I continued in the practice of worship, endeavouring to give a rational explanation of those rites which at first sight were repugnant to me.

At the beginning of our relations, I had no need to do myself any violence. At the time to which I refer [1860?] no one in Spain occupied himself with religion, except in so far as it was related to politics; but people did not for that reason cease to call themselves catholics, although frequently that description was not strictly true. Besides, I had formed the habit of not speaking to anyone on this subject, principally because it was hardly possible to find anyone to talk to except fanatics or Voltaireans....[1]

The imaginary testator marries, and has three children, who

[1] *Minuta*, 24.

are brought up religiously. The responsibilities of parenthood give a new gravity to his style, which begins to recall that of Mr Seagrave in *Masterman Ready*, or Mr Robinson, father of the Swiss family of that name.

What was important above all was that they should never believe that their father was irreligious, or that he had consciously ceased to fulfil his duties in the religious sphere. To this end we did not give up uniting in the family circle, as was our habit, for prayer and for reading the gospels or devotional books; but I refrained from assisting in those cases in which there was a question of acts which were completely incompatible with my convictions.

In establishing this exception, I had in my mind principally *novenas* and the Rosary. I know well that catholicism enjoins reverence for the saints and not adoration; but the truth is that, without the church being able to prevent it, intercession with these is understood in such a way by the faithful that the severe monotheism of the Old Testament and the New have in fact degenerated into a kind of semi-pagan polytheism. As for the Rosary, I have always respected it because it is almost the only religious practice which, in our country, takes place in the bosom of the family; but, considered by itself, it seems absurd to submit to number and measure (by counting the beads) what should be freest, most spontaneous and incapable of coercion of anything in the world: prayer! Every time I see a rosary, there comes to my mind that machine used by the Buddhists of Tibet to measure out and count their prayers and so deduce the merit contracted.[1]

When he surveyed his contemporaries, he saw that in the universities the prevalent opinion was liberal, an opinion rather of sentiment than of reflexion. "Among its adepts were some who, imbued with the principles of the French Encyclopaedists, confounded in the same antipathy both absolutism and religion; while others believed sincerely in the possible harmony of catholicism and liberty."

I was among the latter; and so it was that, catholic or liberal, it seemed to me that the cause of theocracy was distinct from that of the

[1] *Minuta*, 56–8.

Church, and I even expected that the destruction of the former would be to the profit and glory of the latter. As time went by, and the question between the two was brought out more clearly every day, I studied with ardour the works of the so-called liberal catholics of France and Belgium; and although they neither satisfied me nor drew me from my doubts (which now passed to the most fundamental considerations), this school of thought was highly sympathetic to me, because I believed that if its tenets could preponderate, catholicism might still be serviceable to the cause of civilization.

This hope was afterwards gradually destroyed, until at last the *Syllabus* came to convince me that if my former companions of the lecture-room had erred in believing that religion was incompatible with liberty, the Church itself had now declared that catholicism was incompatible with modern civilization.

And really (he adds in a note), since the publication of the *Syllabus* and the declaration of the infallibility of the Roman Pontiff, the vanity of their illusions is made clear to those who by means of one subtle distinction after another tried to escape from what was a mere imposition of logic.

After "many watches and much anguish, which more than once cost tears of blood", there came a day in which, examining his conscience, he was able to formulate a profession of faith which in effect approached most nearly to that of the Unitarians. At last he decided to communicate his change of views to his wife, taking as an excuse a controversy which they had been reading in the newspapers over the apostasy of a certain priest. He relates the scene, painful and prolonged, which took place between them; he was careful to point out the difference between one who is converted to another religion, following the development of his own thought, and one who merely apostatizes from his beliefs. His wife, at last, declared that she would go on loving him as before, and the education of his children was continued as it had begun.

The *Minute* has all the character of a thinly veiled psychological autobiography; the profession of faith as "a meeting place for philosophy, positive religion, rationalist theism and protestant Christianity" is Azcárate's own and is repeated and enlarged in the *Philosophical and Political Studies* published in the following year (1877).

The religious ideas of Azcárate (Zulueta observes)[1] underwent no further change. They were firmly formulated in his mind when he was about 33; and once his *Credo* was said, he experienced no doubts and suffered no contradictions. "Although he believed in the immortality of the soul, his own was not always in search of theological solutions. He attended preferably to the conduct of this life, and tried only to do what was right without worrying himself about an unknown hereafter. His religion was a rational and moral Christianity. Doubtless he thought, with St Paul, that of faith, hope and charity, the greatest was charity, *i.e.* love and justice."

In politics he maintained the secular, lay position; but out of respect to religion and to law he was always ready to defend liberty of conscience and liberty of worship. "In his Christianity there prevailed the ethical aspect, the same note of balance, serenity and reason which dominated the whole of his character. He was no mystic, no spirit tortured by riddles eternally insoluble." But in his own village of Villimer he went to church. It was in a quiet, green country of elms and orchards, not far from León—a country giving a very different impression from the dramatic austerity of Castille where there are only two answers to a question; yes or no. The village lies on the way to the unique and curious horse-shoe arched church of San Miguel de Escalada, built in a Muslim style by Christian monks who had fled from Córdoba in the tenth century. The church at Villimer is a far humbler and less notable edifice; but it was restored by Azcárate himself, and he was present at the service of dedication. Such a man was obviously a reader of Balfour's *Foundations of Belief*; that and Seeley's *Ecce Homo* were among his bed-books. But his constant companion was a Spanish New Testament printed in 1836 for George Borrow, or under his influence, and a "text" (which also he had carried with him from his earliest years), a little picture of a cross with a few pale wild flowers, and a verse from one of the Gospels, in English.

[1] *La oración del incrédulo*, 255, 257–8.

Azcárate was a man with a strong social conscience; a Christian, although he could not remain within the Roman Catholic Church. He was essentially a man of his time, brought up partly on the principles of nineteenth-century English liberalism and partly on the doctrines of Krause, which, reconstructed in Spain under the influence of Sanz del Río, Giner de los Ríos and Azcárate himself, constitute a philosophy of liberty with an ethical motive,

a form of liberty with the obligation to transform the State into a juristic order of positive action, which neither can nor ought to remain indifferent to social suffering and injustice.[1]

Under the influence of Spanish Krausism and the philosophical liberty which it brought, Azcárate endeavoured to harmonize the needs of a liberal régime (the rights of man, constitutional guarantees and liberties) with the exigencies of social justice which demand a calculated and efficient intervention of the State. As an active sociologist and a convincing speaker, he made his influence felt in the Cortes and his later writings are related to his experiences of parliamentary life. Azcárate had always been an untiring defender of constitutional practice and the efficacy of parliamentary action, the outspoken enemy of the corrupt practices which, in the Spain of the Restoration, did so much to discredit it.

He was a life-long apostle of the political ideals of free peoples, and of the close connexion between politics and ethics by means of Law (or Right)—of all, that is to say, which the late dictatorship denied, ignored and assaulted.[2]

The professor of comparative legislation in the University of Madrid was an influential writer on moral and political science; he published a history of the law of property in Spain, and other works including *Parliamentary Institutions in Practice* and *Self-government and the Doctrinaire Monarchy*. The latter, with a clear vision of the future, brought out the incompatibility of

[1] A. Posada, introduction to Azcárate's *Régimen parlamentario en la práctica*, new ed. (1932).
[2] *Ibid.*

doctrinaire monarchy as it was known in Spain with the principle of self-government; and it is worthy of note that it was written in 1877, at the beginning of the restoration of the Bourbon dynasty in Spain.

We have tried to show (he concludes), as incompatible with the principles of modern civilization, a doctrinaire monarchy like that of the old régime, both limited (Isabella II) and absolute (Ferdinand VII). But we must also inquire whether the needs of modern life are fulfilled by a type of monarchy which is truly representative, constitutional and parliamentary; whether a republic alone satisfies this imperious necessity; or whether perhaps both forms are acceptable, according to the circumstances of a country, since both Switzerland and the United States are considered free countries under a republic, England, Belgium and Italy under a monarchy.

The omission of France, Holland, the Scandinavian countries (and the inclusion of Italy) are a reminder of the date at which the book was written. What appears from the whole argument is "the profound and sweeping character of the transformation which the Spanish monarchy must undergo, if it wishes to escape certain death"—indeed one of the achievements of Azcárate in his maturity when he had reached his position of greatest authority as a parliamentarian, was "to rectify, destroy or scatter" the surviving prejudices in favour of absolute monarchy in Spain—and more especially in the Constitution of 1876—

so that a régime of distrust and lack of confidence might eventually be transformed without violence into one which was representative, democratic and free from the traditional obstacles.

But disillusion had set in from the first. Even in the *Minute of a Testament* he had written:

The Restoration began in the inspiration of sentiments of toleration and a spirit of expansion; but every day it contradicted those aims which it had proclaimed at the beginning. I believe that a kind of fatality prevents this dynasty from being able to solve the social and political problems which are arising at the present time; and as it is an illusion to think that any monarchy is possible in Spain except that of the Bourbons, I consider that the only form of government likely to provide the solution is a Republic.[1]

Yet there were moments when another solution seemed possible. After the passing of the British Parliament Act in 1911, people in Spain began to think that if there were really to be a renovation in Spanish political life, the urgent thing was not, perhaps, the immediate establishment of a republic after all. Without going so far as that, there were many things which ought to be done, and could be done, with only one essential condition: the monarchic spirit and the prejudices which found their support in the monarchy must no longer be an obstacle or brake on the democratic, juristic and social reforms which ought to be introduced as soon as possible.[2]

This was the significance of a movement initiated by Azcárate and supported by a group of men, some republicans, others monarchists, and others again who were indifferent to the form of the State. These men were in agreement on four points. (1) There was at the moment no current of opinion strong enough to make possible a change of government to a republic. (2) The immediate benefit which might result from a "surgical operation" would hardly compensate for the inevitable confusion which it would produce. Castelar had said that a civil list was cheaper than a civil war, and a revolution, however successful, would prove costly—it would be better to meet it half-way or avoid it altogether. (3) The main thing was to propose a serious, democratic policy—above all, the secularization of the State, which was regarded as a fundamental requisite; to change a régime of limited toleration for religious beliefs into one of full liberty of conscience. (4) There was also the constitutional reform of the Senate—a real traditional obstacle—and the creation of a national education, which should be modern, free and in the hands of laymen, and should bring culture within the reach of all Spanish subjects. The conditions demanded by republicans for their support of a constitutional monarchy were that there should be no opposi-

---

[1] *Minuta de un testamento*, 84.
[2] A. Posada, *España en crisis* (1923), 101.

tion on the part of the "obstacles" themselves: there must be no interference in the business of the State from the old monarchic spirit or from the confessional spirit stirred up by the religious orders.

It is worth going fully into these proposals of 1911 and 1912, because they show that there was actually an idea of achieving, by means of a truly constitutional monarchy "in the English style", those very reforms for which the Second Republic has been most bitterly attacked—those relating to lay education and the control of the religious orders. These reforms have always been regarded in Spain as of fundamental importance, and no amount of propaganda—particularly in England—should blind us to the fact that they represent the legitimate and long-standing aspirations of what would be a majority of the Spanish people, if to vote liberal were not condemned as a deadly sin.

In the days when this movement began to take shape in Spain—as a result of the passing of the Parliament Act in Great Britain—reform was so much in the air that even the advisers of King Alfonso thought it opportune for the monarch to make a gesture. "The venerable Azcárate, incarnation of the highest civic virtues, could accept their invitation without violence to his old republican conscience and without altering by a single hair's breadth the whole significance of his career." He drove to the Palace in a cab, wearing a top-hat and an immense fur coat, and entered the royal presence, appearing, in face and manner, like the Spanish commander in Velázquez's picture, receiving the keys of Breda. The traditional obstacles seemed to have disappeared! Azcárate left the Palace as republican as when he entered it; but as time went by it became obvious that the "obstacles" were still there, and that the only chance of removing them was to remove the monarchy itself.

The monarchy made one false step after another: the Moroccan disaster of 1921 and the casualties which it brought to thousands of poor Spanish homes; the grotesque dictatorship of 1923, with its well-meaning general and his less scrupulous followers, with its dubious speculation in high places and the fortunes made out of foreign concessions; the unrest among university students at privileges given to the religious orders in the vital matter of examinations, and the threat to suppress all those institutions and educational activities which owed their origin to Don Francisco Giner—all these served to turn public opinion definitely against the monarchy and against the person of King Alfonso. The population of Spain had long ceased to take him seriously, either as a king or as a man. The summary execution of Fermín Galán at Jaca destroyed what little sympathy there was left. The republicans saw that their moment had come, and that the "civil list" might safely be abolished now that the chances of civil war seemed more than usually remote. They staked their chances on the large republican majorities in the municipal elections; and the monarchy went down at once, the captain being the first to leave the sinking ship. It was not quite *spurlos gesenkt*, however, as it was in Portugal. The republicans were too generous in their hour of triumph. Instead of suppressing the religious orders, they legalized them and gave them votes, with the result that the veto of the "traditional obstacles" remained as before.

Azcárate preferred the methods of persuasion and evolution to the more violent "surgical" methods. It was largely through his influence that, at the time of the judicial murder of Francisco Ferrer in 1909, Pablo Iglesias and the socialists were persuaded to abandon their policy of non-co-operation with the republicans and form the alliance which brought in the Second Republic.[1] He conceived the parliamentary machine as being the most adequate mechanism for giving effect to public opinion; but, as one of its stoutest defenders, he saw with indignation the corrupt practices of the so-called *parlamentarismo*, a degeneration of the parliamentary machine through practices which, more than anything else, had contributed to the discredit of the parliamentary system. Although written as long ago as 1885, his book on this subject contains many ideas which still apply to modern conditions; for the doubts which have led to dictatorships are not only doubts in the efficacy of Parliament, but attacks on all representative institutions.

[1] J. J. Morato, *Pablo Iglesias*, 186.

Only those who lived and worked with Azcárate as social reformers in Spain know what he achieved in constructive labour legislation, and in bringing together classes which are generally hostile and often in open war with one another owing to their views on direct action.[1] Certain tendencies in Spain towards moderation, a serenity of outlook and vigilant co-operation in social reform by parliamentary action, are owing, to a large extent, to the influence of Azcárate from the presidential chair of the Institute of Social Reform, which he founded in 1903, and directed with masterly tact up to the day of his death in 1917.

The following example of Azcárate's personal ascendency is related by Posada; it occurred during the strike at Río Tinto in 1914. Azcárate was president of the commission of mediation and arbitration which was trying to solve the problem. The *gran anciano*—Azcárate too had come to be the "grand old man" of Spain—the *gran anciano* had worked untiringly on the commission; there were sittings of four, five and six hours, and even longer. One night the commission sat until 3 a.m. debating one of the miners' claims which the mediators accepted and the owners refused. At last a representative of the owners broke off the discussion: "*Señores*, we give in! We give in as proof of our respect and consideration for our illustrious chairman, who presides over us with such unfailing good temper and never shows the least sign of weariness. And at this time of night, too! No: that's enough! we give in!" An agreement was reached.[2]

Azcárate, with his courtly "Velazquenian" manner and his unwearying patience, combined with a certain patrician, faintly military bearing, made it impossible for anyone in his presence to talk nonsense or play the fool. Azcárate was the ideal chairman; in fact it might be said that he died in the chair. On 13th December, 1917, he was about to preside over a meeting of the Institute of Social Reform. Feeling unwell he intended that afternoon to resign in favour of the vice-president, the Vizconde de Eza, whom he himself had proposed as his

[1] Posada, Introduction to Azcárate's *Régimen parlamentario en la práctica*, 8.
[2] *Ibid.* 9.

successor. Azcárate came up to the table and sat down. He prepared to read a document which had just been put into his hands—a letter in which the workmen's representatives regretfully announced their resignation until such time as the government should set free those who were in prison as a result of the strike of August, 1917, among them Largo Caballero, afterwards a member of the Republican Cabinet. Azcárate tried to unfold the typewritten protest from the workmen's representatives, but his fingers failed him. He leaned heavily to one side; he tried to reach the president's bell. . . .

Azcárate had performed the last act of his public life.

XI

COSSÍO
or the Day's Work

IN 1914 an unusual series of lectures was given at Madrid. The impulse came from the students themselves—men and women who were training to be teachers. They suggested the names of the lecturers and the subject which most interested them: the call to the national spirit which had been made by such men as Costa, Cajal, Unamuno, Azorín—the protest against discouragement made by the "Generation of 1898". Among the lecturers invited was Cossío; the drift of his discourse has been preserved from notes taken by a Portuguese teacher who was present, and published a few days afterwards in a Lisbon newspaper.[1]

Cossío, though an admirable lecturer, had begun to have a feeling of doubt, almost of repugnance, so far as lectures were concerned; doubt as to their practical use, doubt whether they really had any value at all. On that occasion (he said) they had all come together as persons already convinced; they were all persons who could read. Why then go to lectures? There was a great difference between listening and reading. Listening was often sheer waste of time; reading was worth much more. There was something in the air of a lecture-room which often spoilt the effect which a lecture was meant to produce. What they wanted was doing, not talking. The essential thing was to teach people to read. Books brought ideas with them. The centre of gravity of the Spanish problem could be determined thus: Read; possess books. What was a country where there were no books? Education was outlined by literature, by books; and from that came the necessity for schools. Instead of giving lectures, it would be better to teach people to read; to promote by all means the extension, the universality of reading. Were they on the way to the Spanish people being able to read? The

[1] (Alice Pestana), *Diario de Noticias*, 20 March, 1914.

figures for illiteracy were appalling. He would not say that they had lost faith in ideals; what they had lost faith in was men, and without men—reliable men and women—nothing could be done in the way of social work that was good and lasting. What was to be done, then? First find the men. They did not exist? Then make them as quickly as possible, stretch out a helping hand to the young; choose the best; work quietly but quickly. Then again the best teachers should be sent to the most remote and wretched villages. Nothing about seniority and categories! Every teacher was a member of the *Universitas*, the University in the widest sense, and to every teacher, without distinction of category, they entrusted the same charge for the same purpose; they handed him the child to be educated, to be made into a man, or a woman. Such, more or less, was what Cossío said at the Ateneo de Madrid in 1914; and it is no exaggeration to say that such reforms and improvements in Spanish schools as it was possible to introduce during the reign of Alfonso XIII were all due to Sr Cossío.

If Spanish children to-day have better schools and better teachers than before, we owe it to Cossío. If Spanish children are healthier, happier and better taught, Cossío is responsible. If the young people of to-day enjoy greater liberty and consideration with older men and women, it is all due to Cossío. His teaching and his pupils are to be found in all centres of education, from the most modest country school to the most pretentious college, even those on the other side, who thought themselves safe from his influence. The result has been that already several generations have been freed from the oppression and torment which the earlier generations once suffered.[1]

Don Manuel B. Cossío was one of the earliest of the "Wandering Scholars", described in another chapter, who set out from Spain and became acquainted with the teaching of other countries. He belongs to the group of men and women who gathered round Don Francisco Giner and have been accomplishing "the deepest and most thorough revolution which Spain has yet undergone: the educational revolution". To Sr Cossío

[1] L. Luzuriaga, *Crisol*, 3 October, 1931.

more than to any other man is due the improvement which has been achieved in methods of teaching. From his study at the Museo Pedagógico, he was for forty years the soul and inspiration of public instruction in Spain; the good which has been done—often in the face of obstacles which seemed insurmountable—is due entirely to his devotion, his knowledge of men and his patience.

In politics, he was a member of that generation of republicans who sacrificed everything to union in face of the enemy. Nowadays (it is said) the enemy is no longer the monarchy, or the military dictatorship; nor even the possibility of reaction developing along the lines of clericalism or fascism. It is rather disunion and disloyalty among the republicans themselves; and Cossío still "struggles for fraternity in the republican ranks", still endeavours by his influence to hold the republican forces together in peace and common sense. The Republic may not be beyond criticism; but it is better—both for Spain and for the rest of Europe—than any other possible solution, tending towards the extreme right or the extreme left.

The proclamation of the Republic in April, 1931, found Cossío abroad, seeking to cure a troublesome and painful infirmity. He returned post-haste, half cured, to be near what was going on, without being able actually to take part in it. The spectacle of an enthusiastic but disciplined Spain which greeted him on his return was (he knew) the work of Francisco Giner and Pablo Iglesias, the result of education in the school and education among the masses. The country was interested, before everything, in two questions: land and schools, just as had been foreseen by Costa, and indeed by Cossío himself; for it was Cossío who actually drafted Costa's programme for him, and wrote it down at Don Francisco's dictation, while Costa stumped the country defending it. In the first enthusiasm for the Republic, Cossío was the man of the moment; he would have been elected president, had his health permitted it.

Cossío belongs to the select minority created by the *Institución Libre de Enseñanza*. The Institution, as shown in a previous chapter, has been a vaccine injected into the body of

Spain; it has not itself grown into the *Residencia* or into any of the other bodies created through its influence, though it has been the cause of their growth. It never possessed a definite system of education which could be introduced by decree throughout the country. It has been, rather, a prolonged experiment, perpetually going on; a direction, an aim, a tendency; a reform which is never finished, "a perpetual example of the most daring educational principles faced by practical reality". It is not "anti-God"; yet it does not take its orders from Rome. Like the Society of Friends, it will always be a minority; but for fifty years it has been the most active ferment of renewal, the most important door through which modern thought could penetrate into Spain.

Let us examine Cossío's "day's work" in education, from one end of the scale to the other, from the university to the elementary school. Needless to say, he has never been impressed by the devout philistinism which proclaims illiteracy to be a state of grace, and more particularly a saving grace of the Spanish people. Illiteracy, as he knew, is no more a defence against a tendencious press than inaccessibility is against oratory or broadcasting. His lecture at the Athenaeum makes that quite clear. But he saw that educational reform in Spain should begin at the top; the "governing classes" were relatively more ignorant than the governed, and the politicians and political journalists more in need of education than the people.

The urgent problem confronting us to-day (Cossío wrote in 1879) is to avoid the melancholy spectacle of young men who reach the universities without knowing how to listen, or think, or say what they think.[1]

Since these words were written, the spirit of the Spanish universities has been gradually transformed. The fall of the dictatorship (which prepared the way for that of the monarchy) was in a great measure the work of university men; while attempts to spread fascism among the students have so far failed. The philosophical attitude originally known as

[1] *De su jornada*, 16.

Krausism has been modified by Giner and his followers, to signify a true "philosophy of liberty"; and this was given practical and political form in a recognition of certain fundamental necessities, ethical and juristic. The object—and, in a large measure, the achievement—of the "Institutionists" has been to produce men: persons capable of conceiving an ideal and of governing both their own lives and the lives of others, and of doing so by the harmonious employment of all their faculties.[1]

One of the great ideas of Cossío has been "to bring the university to the elementary school". We shall see at the end of this chapter one way in which that is now being accomplished. The first and more immediate way was the training of teachers, the endeavour to get the right men and women to adopt that profession. Cossío had heard of a young woman in England who was hesitating whether to become a teacher or a manicurist; there was no room for such people in the teaching profession in Spain.

Cossío's "day's work" has naturally been concerned to a large extent with methods. He has endeavoured, by travel and study, to find or devise ways of teaching which would achieve results in conformity with the ideals of Don Francisco Giner. The following example shows how the Institution faced the problem of teaching history.

We begin (Cossío wrote to a historian in 1904), as with all other subjects, in the lowest grade of the elementary school. The keen interest which children show (even before they can talk) in what has actually happened, for the facts and the way they are related—the intense pleasure which they take in a story—all show how natural to them is the historical sense and how necessary it is to cultivate it from a very early age. Education sets out along the same road which humanity has followed spontaneously and the historian by reflexion—the only road to history—by going to the sources and attending first of all and for a considerable time to the collection of materials. The most important materials are those which appeal to the imagination:

[1] *De su jornada*, 19.

objects, traces of human activity, striking facts; museums of art and antiquities; the narratives of historians and travellers, biographies; photographs of objects, persons and places; representations of historical events. To awake reflexion and stimulate a taste for historical investigation, exercises are given to the children on memories of their own lives, or on events which they have seen or heard of. All this is done, in the first period, in an unsystematic and fragmentary way, without trying to discover the internal relations of facts and things, without binding events together or trying to trace the slightest sketch of a general picture of a people or an epoch, and still less the relationship of all these in the process of history.

This, as will readily be seen, has from the beginning the character of a history of culture. That is not only because it is not confined to mere political history, but also because, in the presence of objects and pictures, more is said of peoples than of persons, thus awakening the idea (without definitely formulating it) that everything is done by everybody, and that the true subject of history is not the hero, but the entire people whose joint labour produces civilization. It is left to the tact of the teacher to choose the occasions most appropriate for showing the relations between historical facts and visible objects, and thus introducing elements of order and system into the teaching of history. A beginning is made by calling attention to the most striking differences shown by the different levels of culture among different peoples; and history gradually comes to mean an account of the efforts which men have made to pass from one state of culture to another. Eventually the treatment becomes more systematic, fixing by contrast the culminating moments in history, *e.g.* Greek civilization of the fifth and fourth centuries B.C., and Christian from the thirteenth century to the fifteenth. Nothing strikes the eye so much as the contrast between a Greek temple and a Gothic cathedral, radically different in appearance and structure, and, for that reason, easily understood by children. And, since art speaks so directly to the imagination, it may be used—especially architecture—as something on which to concentrate the attention and fix the different periods of history in the mind. Thus Romanesque (and Norman) architecture goes with the feudal system, Gothic with the age of corporations and municipalities and the rise of the "third estate". Renaissance architecture with its Graeco-Roman and Baroque developments is associated with the rise of absolute monarchies; while Neo-classicism is the art of enlightened despotism and revolution; and modern art, in its indecision and its eclecticism and its great steel constructions, belongs to the age of democracy with its socialist and libertarian aspirations. Thus the plastic arts may be made the basis for fixing historical relations systematically, and for demonstrating the unbroken development of culture throughout the ages. Art brings home to the child as nothing else can that every change has its necessary antecedents in what has gone before; that ideas change more quickly than forms, that the process of perfection consists in finding forms adequate to ideas, and that in both forms and ideas there always remains a substantial basis common to what has gone before, although the manifestations of it may be different.[1]

Thus Cossío put his master's precepts into practice largely by the aid of art. "His aesthetic vision of reality was deeply imbued with an enthusiasm for ethics, though that did not prevent his fine artistic sense from showing through, and enabled him to be at home in the art of all times and particularly the art of his own time and his own country."[2]

The power of looking at things (he wrote in 1879) may be applied not only to the teaching of history and natural science, but also to almost every branch of education and in some measure to all of them.[3] This is, of course, of the first importance in the teaching of drawing; and yet, with characteristic perversity, drawing is often taught by copying other drawings rather than drawing directly from natural objects.

"It may surprise you", he wrote to a teacher who had applied to him for advice, "that although these facts are so evident, the practice of mere copying is in general use. This is

[1] *De su jornada*, 25–30.   [2] Viqueira, II, 457.
[3] *De su jornada*, 8.

due to the same dogmatic influence which has corrupted all education. The teacher, believing himself to be in possession of the truth, considers that the pupil ought not to discover the truth for himself, either because it is useless to waste time in doing so when it is enough to receive it in lessons or in books, or because he considers the child incapable in his early years of finding it out for himself. From this come all the evils of the present system of education based on lectures and text-books which replace two factors essential to knowledge: the thing to be learnt, and the work of the pupil in finding out about it for himself. By the present system, both of these are suppressed. Instead of the thing itself, the child is given the idea (true or false) which another mind has formed of it; he is made to repeat this without caring whether he makes it really his, his natural ability is atrophied, and the result is a deceptive appearance of knowledge which satisfies parents, teachers and employers, while the victim will deplore it later on (if he ever becomes conscious of it) not only through the time lost, but also through the perversion it has wrought in his own natural faculties."[1]

Drawing, Cossío has always considered to be of the utmost importance; he would even prefer to teach it before writing.

Why not postpone writing and begin with drawing? It is much more real, living and concrete to the child's imagination; and one day he will unconsciously find that he can write, for he will have learnt, among the other things which he can draw, to draw the letters.[2]

At the same time he suggested the postponement of the abstract study of grammar until a later period of instruction, and recommended exercises in the spontaneous expression of the child's thought—the method which is now largely employed in the elementary teaching of foreign languages.

Evidence of the power which Giner and Cossío had in teaching their pupils to see, and to realize the existence of art, comes from no less a person than Professor Rafael Altamira.

[1] *De su jornada*, 131.   [2] *Ibid.* 12.

I was an undergraduate in my third year when for the first time in my life a friend of Giner's put me in front of a work of art and made me see how beautiful it was. Up till then, no one, either at school or at the University, had ever given me the faintest suspicion that a picture or a statue, a medieval church or a dado of renaissance tiles could be of importance to my education or widen the horizons of my life. That initiation put me in the position to realize, years after-wards, how great the influence of Don Francisco had been in teaching people in that way. It opened a new world to my intelligence, brought me the greatest intellectual delights, and helped me sub-stantially towards the understanding of history.[1]

This attraction was felt by others, besides Professor Altamira. A number of young men who received that influence were turned to archaeological and artistic studies—witness the young Englishman, Henbest Capper, whose experiences have already been described. The movement also led to the re-discovery of not a few of the artistic treasures of ancient Spain, which had been forgotten or despised until the diligence of Giner, Cossío and their pupils, with their affectionate study and frequent excursions to out-of-the-way places, brought them to the knowledge of the Spanish public. One of the first tasks of the revolution was to ensure that those treasures should be kept in safe custody and not leave the country. So many had already disappeared—sold to dealers and smuggled across the frontier—that it became necessary to consider how the remainder could be preserved in safety. The abuses of the "owners"—religious foundations or churches—had to be limited by administrative police measures; and it became necessary to determine the legal position of that part of the treasure which, utilized as it was in public Catholic worship, was claimed (on most unsound legal arguments) to belong to the patrimony of the Church.[2]

Yet art, as Cossío knew, was not only to be found in the "fine arts". Industrial art had also to be considered; and the popular, traditional art in which Spain has been so fertile and so productive. Don Francisco had paid attention to this subject;

---

[1] *Giner de los Ríos, educador*, 41–2.
[2] *Cuadernos de política*, I, 58.

so also had his brother, Don Hermenegildo, and the Riaños; but it was the Introduction written by Cossío to the Catalogue of a Spanish exhibition of Lace and Embroidery in 1913 that first aroused interest in Spain. The lace and embroidery worked by women—in town and country, in parlours and in kitchens, in girls' schools and convents—are anonymous products, of unequal artistic merit, but employing traditional designs which vary according to the district. Lace-making and embroidery-work have always been deeply rooted in Spanish home life, without distinction of class; and though they are not static but always in process of development, their evolution is as gentle as the slow changes in the face of nature. For popular art—like language, ballads and folk-songs—is an anonymous product, and created in the same way: from the depths of the soul of the people. From this amorphous basis rises at intervals an artist of distinction and an aristocratic art. Differentiations are produced; schools; the transference of inspiration from one place to another, and the accents peculiar to creative genius. And when all this has come into being, popular art once again is united with it, and nourished by it as mother earth lives and is nourished at the expense of the beings which she brings forth. Thus the higher and purer, more conscious and more universal, "reflective" or "erudite" art may be, so much the more wealth and intensity, so much the more character, is gained by the art of the people, which in the course of nature is able to take all good nourishment into itself and make it native to the soil. As a cloud returns to the sea, so at last, by innumerable paths, all "erudite" art returns to the deep bosom of the common earth, to the womb where it had its origin. But the process of absorption is slow, and requires centuries for its completion; and so we find an exuberance of popular art in the older nations, while the new countries are without it, or only possess it in very small quantity. "Time cannot be improvised, nor can history anticipate the hour."[1]

The study of furniture, pottery, costume, jewelry was not a mere pastime with Cossío and Don Francisco, any more than

[1] *De su jornada*, 328–9.

the study of painting or music. "As to *that*", Don Francisco
would remark, "you know what Sanz del Río used to say of
philosophy; that it gives everyone what he asks from it, and has
something for all tastes."[1]

Music, "the Cinderella of the Arts", was not forgotten at the
Institution; indeed she was treated strictly on an equality with
her other sisters. Giner had urged the establishment of classes of
musical aesthetics and musical history in the Conservatoire.
They had been founded by the First Republic; but by 1878
nothing had yet been done in Madrid, though the flourishing
school of music in Cadiz—the birth-place, incidentally, of
Manuel de Falla—could provide classes in acoustics, aesthetics,
the history of music and general history of the fine arts. The
Conservatoire at Madrid took some time to catch up with the
Academia de Santa Cecilia at Cadiz.

Was it a natural thing (Don Francisco asked ironically) for
musicians not to know the history of their art, either theoretically or
practically? Not to know which were the great works, the character
and style of the music of different ages—a thing which, modestly
enough, but with great applause, had been taught and illustrated at
the *Institución Libre de Enseñanza*?...How was the performer ever to
interpret the works of other times, without knowing about their
culture, their style and their attitude to life; without living them and
expressing them in his playing?...That was the reason why we
frequently had to suffer from an insipid performance, or one which
completely destroyed the character of a composition—a minuet of
Haydn in which an ill-advised pianist would develop a sonority
proper to one of the stupendous Fantasies of Thalberg or Liszt, or
fade away in the plaintive tones of a Nocturne of Chopin.[2]

The greatest triumph of the ideal of Cossío—the crown of
fifty years of work by Don Francisco and the Free Institution—
has been the formation of *Misiones pedagógicas*. Their purpose is
best described in their founder's own words: "a travelling
school, going from place to place; but a school in which there
are no school-books, where learning is without tears, where no

[1] *Estudios de artes industriales*, 2.   [2] *Ibid.* 225.

one has to kneel down (as we used to do) and no one wants to play truant".[1]

These "missions" have been sent by the government of the republic to the poorest, most remote and most abandoned villages—to some of those hundreds of villages in Spain in which neither the Church nor the State nor the absentee landlord has ever done a single thing for the welfare of the inhabitants. The new lay *Misiones* have come in the first place to entertain, to amuse; "we should like to entertain you", they explain, "as much as you are entertained by play-actors and puppet-shows. This recreation-school is for everyone, big and little; for those who spend their lives working, for those who never went to school, and for those who have never been near a school since they were children. In the towns, young and old, however humble they may be, have plenty of chances to go on learning all their lives, and to enjoy themselves as well, because they live in the midst of other men better instructed than they are, and have everything at hand, so that instruction and amusement come to them whether they like it or not, through their eyes and ears; for even shop-windows are full of amusement and instruction". Since villages are without these things, the Republican government has undertaken an experiment to see whether it is possible to undo some of the injustice of its predecessors, and has sent little groups of men—chiefly university men and "Residentes"—to talk to remote villagers, to show them paintings and films, and make music for them, and endeavour in a general way to make the hard, barbarous and neglected life of a remote Spanish village more cheerful. "The western world", as Lord Eustace Percy has said, "has re-discovered in the twentieth century the ancient truth that the business of popular education is neither formal teaching nor political enlightenment, but direct social reconstruction."

Part of the "Misión" consists of a travelling art-gallery, containing copies, in approximately the original size, of fourteen celebrated pictures in the Prado Museum, and as many en-

[1] *Residencia*, February, 1933.

gravings.[1] This selection has been made in view of people who have never been away from the remote villages in which they live, or have only been as far as the nearest country towns where there are no museums (although, as the Director of Fine Arts remarked, there is enough "stuff" in Spain, in spite of what has been sold or smuggled out of the country, to make an excellent art-gallery in every provincial capital). The villagers may have seen photographs or coloured reproductions; but they have never seen real pictures nor do they know the look of any painting by one of the great masters. The "Misiones" would like to bring this travelling art-gallery even to the villages most difficult of access, to the "disinherited". But paintings are not like books, the gramophone or the cinema; they are difficult to transport where there is no road, and still more difficult to display where there is no large room in which pictures may be hung in a good light with an appropriate background. So for the present the travelling museum is generally on view at a country town, or a village where there are facilities for installing it. It is accompanied, of course, by persons responsible for hanging the pictures and looking after them, who try to arouse interest by simple explanations and talks on their artistic and historical significance, and sometimes illustrate them with lantern-slides and public talks. On leaving the district, the Museum leaves photographs of all the pictures exhibited, to hang in the village hall or school house, as well as smaller photographs which are distributed free to anyone who asks for them.

The *misioneros* have interesting stories to tell of their experiences, in remote, forgotten villages.

The only public room, as a rule, was the Dancing Hall, the *Salón de baile*, usually a large granary, with an earthen floor and a sort of

---

[1] The paintings are: Berruguete *Auto de Fé*, El Greco *The Resurrection* and *Portrait of an unknown man*, Sánchez Cuello *Prince Carlos*, Ribera *Jacob*, Zurbarán *The Vision of St Peter*, Velázquez *The Tapestry Weavers*, *The Infanta Margarita* and *The dwarf Don Antonio the Englishman*, Murillo *El niño Dios Pastor* and *St Elizabeth of Hungary*, Goya *Shooting the prisoners*, *La Maja vestida* and *El Pelele*.

shed for the musicians where we installed the cinema. There was next to no ventilation, no seats, and absolutely no system of heating. It was bad for our type of work. More than five hundred persons were present, young and old, all wearing mufflers and *berets* and many of them smoking. Mothers, daughters and grandmothers came in increasing numbers every day, and stood for the whole performance. A few—very few—sat on benches which they had brought in from the church; they could not bring chairs from their houses (as they do for puppet-shows) because fewer people would have been able to get in, and there might have been a disturbance. These were the conditions under which we had to work.[1]

There is no doubt that the cinema is the most powerful aid to the work of the *Misiones*. People cannot resist it, even on occasions in which indifference, country suspicion, or an atmosphere of prejudice opposes some difficulty to the cordial welcome with which most villagers have received the lay *misioneros*. Sometimes the houses are on the side of a mountain, difficult of access. The lorry can go no farther. The journey has to be continued on horse or mule, by steep paths and narrow passes. There comes a moment when even a horse can go no farther; all sign of a path disappears, and the broken, slippery ground is dangerous to animals. The men have to go forward on foot, carrying in their hands or on their backs the cases of books, the gramophone, records, cinema and accumulators. At Caín, for instance, a hamlet in the province of León, the place is so precipitous that there is a saying in those parts that the people of Caín die by falling over the edge (*Los de Caín mueren despeñados*). A *misión* went there all the same.

The curiosity of the inhabitants—expectant and at times suspicious—accompanies the *misioneros* as they install themselves in the village square or some other suitable place. The *alcalde* and the school-master, both enthusiastic supporters, help to produce silence enough for the speakers to be heard with a certain amount of comfort. In the intervals they put on records of folk-songs; *cantares* from Asturias or *aires* from Galicia.

[1] *Residencia*, February, 1933.

"What do the *misioneros* bring? Talks, books, films and music. Talks—in a familiar, friendly tone—on a number of pleasant subjects. Attractive books, leading on to great authors. Instructive and amusing films. And in everything that is done there is a feeling of simplicity, of sensibility, of fine comprehension of what it all means and what it ought to be."[1]

When the *misión* leaves a village, it leaves behind it a library of about a hundred volumes, as well as a gramophone and a number of records. The music preferred in the places which the *misiones* have reached so far has been folk-song: records typical of the country.

Thanks to the *misiones*, some villages have made their first acquaintance with electric light. In places where there was none, the *misiones* had to bring their own accumulators. "An enormous sensation, not likely to be forgotten, seeing for the first time in the darkness and silence of the country the prodigy of electric light.... That curious little apparatus which gives an entirely new kind of light, and that other one, the box out of which come voices and music. Men and women looked at one another in amazement. What could that be? Was it witchcraft, devilry? The impression was so vivid that through the minds of the lay *misioneros* there passed from time to time the thought that these people might turn against them, thinking that it was all miracle-mongering and enchantment."

The origin and inspiration of these lay "missions" came from Cossío. He might deny it, and hand back the wreath to Don Francisco, who, in turn, would pass it on to Sanz del Río. Yet there is nothing in contemporary Spain which so bears the imprint of his genius, and nothing, it might be added, which has so roused the scorn and fury of the opposition. Lay "missions"! Pedagogics! Copies of pictures! How absurd, when it is so clearly to the advantage of all concerned that Spanish village-life should remain uncared-for, barbarous and illiterate!

Cossío has expressed himself more completely in the written word than his master, Don Francisco, had ever done. There is, for instance, his admirable *Life* of El Greco—the first to be

[1] *Nuevo mundo,* 19 May, 1933.

published, and the book upon which all biographers and art-critics have freely drawn. Extracts from this and all his published writings were collected in a small volume on the occasion of his retirement in February, 1929: "De su jornada" (From his day's work); it is the *livre de chevet* of every student of modern Spanish things.

But the spirit of Cossío refuses to be confined. It is not wholly in the books which he has published, nor in the lectures given before large audiences, nor even in his classes nor his reports to the Spanish Board of Education. "In all these manifestations of his spirit is undoubtedly to be found something of the real Cossío. Yet where he abandons himself with all the fervour of renaissance enthusiasm is in conversation." To have partaken of that is indeed a privilege; conversation in intimate surroundings with him is one of the greatest experiences in modern Spain.

Salvador Rueda the poet (1857–1933) was a man of picturesque phrase and vehement expression. He was once asked about Cossío.

Cossío? I should just think so! If you'd only seen him with me in the museum, stopping before the things and talking about the sculpture! How he trembled with enthusiasm! You've seen those birds with a feather on their wings which flutters as they sing? Well, that man, when he talked, made even the threads in his coat flutter with excitement!

EPILOGUE

ENGLISH readers, if they have followed thus far the path of the Spanish Reformers of 1868, must have noticed now and again an echo of something which they will have heard before. Though the English influences on the group have been pointed out (as have the French influences on Spanish republicanism and the German influences on Spanish philosophy), the echo of ideas which seem to be "English" cannot be explained away as mere influence. Anyone to-day who reads Giner, Cossío or Azcárate will recognize in them something of the liberal and ascetic creed of the best of his own schoolmasters; for Giner and Cossío were, first and last and above all, excellent schoolmasters who would have been valuable in this or any other country but were more valuable than ever in their own, where until lately the good schoolmaster was liable to prosecution.

For these reasons, ideas like those of the Spanish Reformers of 1868 can sometimes be found in the writings of English contemporaries with whom they had no direct contact. They may be found, for instance, without leaving the precincts of Cambridge.

"I can't make you geologists", Adam Sedgwick would say, "but I can fire your imaginations." And Montagu Butler, the late Master of Trinity, urging the importance of the spirit and the necessity for intellectual enthusiasm, would ask:

"Is it with the prudential calculation of self-interest or with the lover-like transport of affection? Do you love it for what it gives, or for what it is?"

No less might the "eager intellectual brotherhood" of which Don Francisco was the acknowledged centre have heard him speak with unwonted bitterness of "intellectual infidelity, the gradual loss of faith in the higher things of the mind".

Even more appropriate, more true to the Spanish Reformers, are the words in which Frederic William Maitland commemorated Henry Sidgwick. Like Sidgwick, Giner was deeply attached to intimate friends "to whom he unbosomed himself without reserve"; while acquaintances who stood outside that innermost circle had evidence of the keen interest that he took in all manner of human affairs. Men who seemed less self-conscious or less self-centred than Sidgwick or Giner were not to be met, nor any others "who to all appearances so steadily and so easily kept themselves at an objective point of view". And this, though it might have been said of Sidgwick as of Giner that he administered prodigally the holy sacrament of the word.

"To see with your eyes, to find interest in your interests" seemed to be one of their main objects, while they were amusing and delighting you. Both "genuinely wished to know what all sorts of people thought and felt about all sorts of things"; and each had numerous friends at a distance who admired and honoured him. Don Francisco also was notable (as Sidgwick was) for his "singular truthfulness", and for the way he trained his pupils to severe sincerity. He would have delighted in Sidgwick's insistence on "the exact point where proof ended and only hope remained".

Yet we must not make the mistake made by so many foreign observers of regarding everything fine or admirable or interesting in Spain as being of foreign origin. Even a close Portuguese observer, Dr Fidelino de Figueiredo, can carry away the idea that "there is something foreign and protestant in Don Francisco Giner... the delicate, serene surface of a soul, without the heroic, combative profundities of the soul which is really and truly Spanish, and in which the very virtues themselves hollow out the nest for the defects".[1] His writings (he adds) were "like a mirror held up to contemporary life as it ran to offer its image"; but he denies him all originality, all "definite achievement", and in all his works he can find "not a single page which is definitely Spanish".

Perhaps it takes an Englishman to see how definitely, how intensely Spanish Don Francisco was.

That little man with his gentle manners, "concealing behind

[1] *Las dos Españas*, 231.

his smile and his grey hairs an unsuspected tenacity of purpose", the reformer who was "far more to be dreaded than the ingenuous republicans of 1868", the apostle who appeared to some as the founder of a new heretical sect—"a sort of exotic protestantism"—and was condemned as the "de-christianizer" and "de-hispanizer" of Spain, was in actual fact one of the most Spanish figures which modern Spain has produced. German philosophy and English ways of living had been an inspiration to him, just as the French political ideals of 1789 and 1871 proved an inspiration to some of his friends; but the basis of Don Francisco's thought was deeply rooted in the soil of Spain.

"This fine flower of Spanish thought", Azorín writes, in one of his lectures on Spanish landscape, "could not have been produced without a deeply-laid tradition in which the seed could take root. That part which seems to us foreign was in fact profoundly and intimately national. When we consider his philosophy—it is more than a philosophy—we seem to see, reaching forward into it, living again in it, many ideas which are traditionally Spanish". We see them, for instance, in Melchor Cano in the sixteenth century, with his demand for independence and civil liberty, and in the eighteenth century in Campomanes, with his insistence on the conscious dignity of the worker, and in the delightful "Moroccan Letters" of Cadalso with their criticism of accepted Spanish values.

Don Francisco brought not only a philosophy but a whole attitude to life (which is what a philosophy should be); but it was an attitude which, if it was unusual in the Spain of his time, was nevertheless an attitude which has always been maintained by some of the choicest spirits in Spain.

"Encouraging masters, wise counsellors, delightful companions"; able, appreciative and affectionate. Life was not frivolous, or tragical or hateful; but it was serious. *Humanas actiones*—Don Francisco was fond of quoting Spinoza—*non ridere, non lugere neque detestari, sed intelligere*.

INDEX